QUILTS FROM EUROPE

PROJECTS AND INSPIRATION

GÜL LAPORTE

C&T PUBLISHING

©2000 Gül Laporte
Illustrations ©2000 C&T Publishing, Inc.

Editor: Liz Aneloski
Technical Editor: Beate Nellemann
Copy Editor: Steve Cook
Cover Designer: Christina Jarumay
Book Designer: Irene Morris, Morris Design
Design Director: Kathy Lee
Illustrator: Richard Sheppard
Published by C&T Publishing, Inc., P.O. Box 1456, Lafayette, California 94549

Front cover (clockwise from upper left):
Reflection (detail) by Dorle Stern-Straeter
Entrance (detail) by Heide Stoll-Weber
Material Thoughts (detail) by Anco Brouwers-Branderhorst
Traboules (detail) by Odile Texier
Back cover:
Rythme by Maryline Collioud-Robert

Attention Teachers: C&T Publishing, Inc. encourages you to use this book as a text for teaching. Contact us at 800-284-1114 or www.ctpub.com for more information about the C&T Teachers Program.

When converting designs originally in metric units, the following conversion
rules have been applied:
1) 1 inch = 2.54 cm.
2) All dimensions have been adjusted to nearest $1/8$ inch as needed to maintain the original shape of the design. In the galleries throughout the book dimensions have been adjusted to the closest centimeter.

Library of Congress Cataloging-in-Publication Data

Laporte, Gul
    Quilts from Europe : projects and inspiration / Gul Laporte.
    p. cm.
  Includes index.
  ISBN 1-57120-095-9 (paper trade)
  1. Patchwork—Europe. 2. Patchwork quilts—Europe. 3.
Quiltmakers—Europe. I. Title.
  TT835 .L35 2000
  746.46'094—dc21
                                    99-6795
                                    CIP

Printed in Hong Kong
10 9 8 7 6 5 4 3 2 1

Contents

Introduction

Sincere thanks
to all the artists
who contributed
to this book
and shared their
knowledge and
inspiration with
us. Also, many
thanks to C&T
for their help
and support.
I would like to
thank especially
Liz Aneloski,
the editor whose
help, support, and
patience I valued
enormously.

Although Europeans probably have Americans to thank for the regeneration of quiltmaking, I believe that Americans are also interested in knowing how Europeans and the rest of the world have interpreted this art, which Americans consider a part of their heritage. This book is intended to show a wide range of innovative traditional and contemporary work executed by well-known European artists. Many have already received international recognition, having exhibited in Japan, the United States (at Visions or Quilt National), and throughout Europe. Some travel in many countries, teaching and lecturing, while others prefer to concentrate on creating new work. With their innovation and creativity, the artists I have chosen are showing a strong influence from their background and experience. Choosing between so many talented European artists has been a difficult task. The colors, fabrics, and embellishments may not be the most popular or well known, but I hope that this book will provide a new source of inspiration to many and give a good idea of what kind of work is currently taking place in Europe. I hope that this book will give you the opportunity to "explore" Europe and discover not only some of the European quilters, but also the traditions from their countries. They are all very honored that their work has been recognized internationally.

32" x 32" (81 cm x 81 cm)

by Gül Laporte

Improvisational work using
hand-dyed and Bali fabrics.
Machine pieced, machine and
hand quilted.

Photo: Gül Laporte

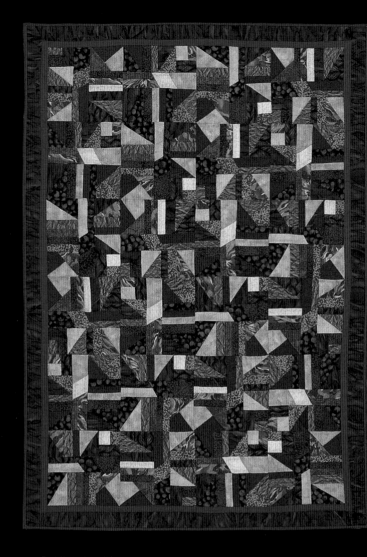

48" x 55" (122 cm x 140 cm)
by Gül Laporte
One block is repeated and
rotated, making the block seem
to disappear. Machine pieced,
hand quilted.

Photo: Gül Laporte

50" x 52" (127 cm x 132 cm)
by Gül Laporte
In this quilt I wanted to
experiment with black and
white. When it was finished,
it reminded me of the buildings
of Manhattan in New York City.
Machine pieced, hand quilted.

Photo: Gül Laporte

EUROPEAN QUILTING TRADITIONS

Although it is not certain how quilting reached Europe from its origins in the Middle and Far East, the British Isles and the Netherlands have a very strong tradition in patchwork and quilting. Quilts can be traced as far back as the 14th century. In the British Isles, records show that quilts were fairly common in the homes of royalty and nobility from the 16th century on. Men had a role in piecing and designing quilts. Soldiers, sailors, and tailors were attracted by the challenge of complicated piecing. Originally, patchwork was not only meant to make warm covers for the bed; it was also used in clothing, shoes, protective shirts, banners, and many other applications. ■ Unfortunately, textiles are fragile and quilts are perishable. In Egypt there are some pieces of patchwork in museums that date back to the first century BC. The oldest piece that can be seen in a German museum is St. Elisabeth's repentance shirt, which dates from the 13th century. However, the kind of patchwork clothing men were wearing at that time can be seen in old books, paintings, drawings, and miniatures. ■ Although patchwork and quilting were imported to the United States by the European immigrants, the tradition of patchwork faded in Germany, the United Kingdom, and the Netherlands. European women didn't have time to spend stitching and quilting by hand during the Industrial Revolution of the 19th century. ■ Some European countries have no quilting tradition whatsoever. France for instance, has no tradition of patchwork, but instead has very strong textile, stitched counterpane, Marseille work, and boutis traditions. ■ In some European countries during the last twenty-five years, quilters have revived their art impressively, thanks to different exhibitions organized by Americans in the United States and internationally. In 1972, when Jonathan Holstein's beautiful quilt collection traveled through Europe, women became very enthusiastic. Many, with no guidance, tried to reproduce some of the beautiful patterns seen during that exhibition. Some fine-arts artists became fascinated with the use of color and the possibilities of expressing themselves through textiles. Most of them started with traditional blocks or patterns, but soon moved on using their own inspirations and discovering different quilting possibilities in their travels.

RENÉE GOSSE

The Artist

Renée Gosse grew up in the Provence region of France, which is known for its sun, colors, and perfumes. She now lives in the suburbs of Paris, in a big charming house full of antique boutis and provençal counterpanes and coverlets. She has a passion for boutis and spends months creating new pieces, carefully following traditional methods. ■ The boutis came about from an evolution that combines quilting, the Marseille stitch, and embossed embroidery. In Marseille work, two fabrics were stitched together following a pattern drawn on the top fabric, which was stuffed. In the 18th century, the surface was covered with very delicate vermicelli stitches and closely embroidered knots adding another texture. In the 19th century patterns were stitched with running stitches and were padded with cotton wool and cording, which became the boutis, a word from Provence, which means "to stuff." ■ Two pieces of boutis, the wedding petticoat and the bedspread, were essential for any bride's trousseau. Boutis works were made for the main events of life: weddings and births. Most of the designs in boutis represent symbols such as: pigeons, roosters, dogs, sheep, melons, artichokes, pomegranates, doves, St. Andrew's cross, the Maltese cross, basket of fruit, cornucopia, children, oak leaves, intertwined hearts, stars, and grapes. ■ Pricked, embossed linens and boutis have come back into fashion and out of linen cupboards. Many ladies in this century of speed dare to spend hours on needlework and boutis, this highly Provençal technique.

Piqûre de Marseille
36" x 28" (90 cm x 70 cm)
Maker unknown.
This Marseille work from the first half of the 18th century is made of cotton and linen. It is embroidered following the backstitching method, popular at that time. Renée Gosse's private collection.
Photo: Guy Yoyotte

The Gallery

L'Arbre d'Ispahan (The Tree of Ispahan)

40" x 40" (102 cm x 102 cm)
Renée got her inspiration from a silk rug she saw in Iran. Once back at her hotel room, she drew some of the designs on a piece of paper and, much later, she decided to make a boutis out of it.

Photo: Guy Yoyotte

Jardin d'Orient (Oriental Garden)

51" x 50" (130 cm x 127 cm)
Partially inspired by a printed calico from the 17th century ("indienne") from the Middle East. Specially made for Expo V in Lyon, France.

Photo: Guy Yoyotte

**Les Fleurs de Mon
Jardin en Provence
(The Flowers from
My Garden in
Provence)**

54" x 64" (137 cm x 163 cm)
Boutis inspired by the flowers
of her garden in Provence.

Photo: Guy Yoyotte

**Immortelle Provence
(Immortal Provence)**

48" x 64" (163 cm x 122 cm)
The traditional designs are
inspired by an antique petticoat.
Renée enlarged some of the
motifs and reproduced them on
this boutis, arranging them
among her own designs.
Made for Expo VI in Innsbruck,
Austria.

Photo: Guy Yoyotte

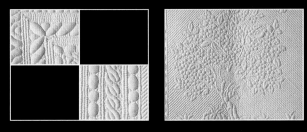  

The Project

Petasson

21" x 19" (53 cm x 48 cm)

This piece of cloth, worked with the boutis method using a 19th century design, was originally used as a pad to lay a baby on your lap.

Its thickness prevented any leaking in the event of an accident.

Photo: Guy Yoyotte

One Quarter of Design

D

M

MI

O

he boutis technique is similar to trapunto. The boutis, which dates to the 18th century, is a completely reversible piece. Here, Renée explains the 19th century traditional technique of stitching and filling the piece.

- Two pieces of white, good-quality, 100% cotton fabric, with unwashed dimensions of 28" x 24" (71 cm x 61 cm) *Fabrics should be at least 10% larger than the finished size. (Do not prewash the fabric. The completed project will be washed to close up the holes left from stuffing. Fabrics that have already been washed will not have the same elasticity.)*
- 1/8 yard (11 cm) for binding
- Fine cotton cording, approximately 6 oz.
- Machine thread DMC #40, 100% cotton
- Cotton batting for the stuffing
- #10 quilting needles and a #18 blunt-end tapestry needle
- Embroidery scissors with sharp points
- Quilting or tapestry hoop
- 20" (50 cm) ruler and a 2H or HB pencil
- Fine wooden manicure stick

Drawing

1. Enlarge the design on page 12, 160%.

Tip: It is easier to trace the complete design on tracing paper before marking the design on the fabric. Rotate design for lower right quadrant and mirror image design for upper right and lower left quadrants.

2. Mark an "O" in the center of one of the pieces of fabric. From O, mark the medians M and M1 as well as the diagonal D.

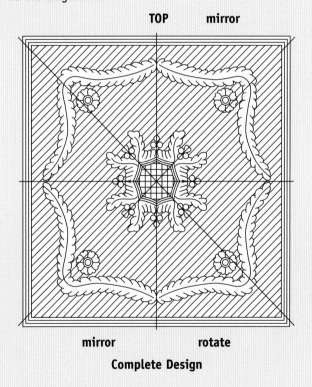

TOP   mirror

mirror   rotate

Complete Design

3. Place the enlarged design under the fabric, matching center and all other marks.

4. Trace the inner design into each quarter.

Trace inner design.

5. Trace the outer design in the same way.

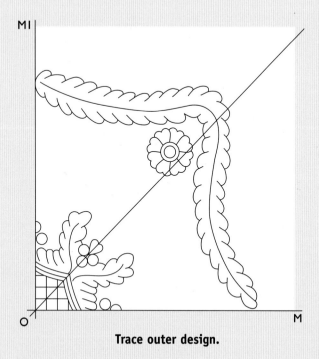

Trace outer design.

6. Trace the four border lines ¹/₄" (6 mm) apart.

Trace border lines.

7. Working from the diagonal line, draw parallel lines at scant ¹/₄" (6 mm) intervals to form channels.

Draw parallel lines from the diagonal line.

Assembly

1. Put the marked fabric on top of the backing fabric, wrong sides together, and baste.

2. Place in the hoop (avoid stretching too tightly).

3. Quilt through both layers around the motifs and along the parallel lines, using small running stitches. Quilt slightly on each side of each center grid line to form a small channel. Slide the knots through and hide them between the two layers. No knots should show on either the back or front of the work.

Filling

Motif Filling

1. Cut batting into strips $1/8$" (3 mm) wide by 8" (20.3 cm) long.

2. When the quilting is complete, begin by stuffing the center design motif from the back of the work. Start from one edge working toward the center. Begin at the tip, filling each leaf section separately as follows: With the wooden stick, part the threads of the fabric without breaking them and gently push in the strips of batting. Take care not to overstuff. With a sharp needle, carefully close the holes as you go.

Note:

■ *You must individually stuff each berry and the petals of the flowers.*

Attention:

■ *Always begin the filling from the edge of the motif.*

Channel Filling

Octagonal Channels

1. Thread two strands of cotton cording into the channel using the blunt tapestry needle.

2. Once the thread is pulled through the channel, trim the thread with the embroidery scissors, cutting as close as possible to the exit and entry points. Be sure to close the needle holes.

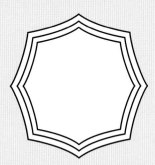

Use two strands of thread.

Center Grid Channels

Use one strand of thread to fill the channels on the center grid.

Diagonal and Border Channels

Use four strands of the thread.

Finishing

1. Finish the work with a thin binding or a narrow hem.

2. Hand wash using cold water and a mild soap. Rinse well, squeeze out excess water, and dry flat. Never iron. For a larger project, enlarge the space between the outer motif and the border channels.

ODILE TEXIER

Odile Texier was born in Lyon, France, the city of silk, and brought up in her cradle with the noise of looms as a lullabye. She can still remember the colorful silk bobbins which filled the Lyon weavers' workshops. She

The Artist

lived in la Croix Rousse, a district of Lyon where houses were built in the 19th century with high ceilings, making them quite suitable for housing power looms. ■ In her quilting, she never makes a drawing first. Instead, she lets the colors and textures guide her along her creative process. As she has always liked geometrical designs better than figurative ones, she enjoys bringing traditional patterns up-to-date and giving them a personal touch with her choice of fabrics. She is drawn to fabrics by their colors and textures, as well as their feel and sparkle. Glistening, rich, bright fabrics such as silk appeal to her—probably due to the influence of her childhood. However, she also likes to use chintzs and commercial fabrics. ■ She doesn't have a studio, but the tiny workshop inside her house is her playground, and she believes that the best cure for life's problems is to be inspired and to create new pieces with the wonderful fabrics she endlessly collects.

Persienne (Shutter)

45" x 65" (114 cm x 165 cm)
In this quilt, Odile wanted to show the softness of the light through the laths of the shutters and to isolate the rays of light from one block to the other. Quilt selected and exhibited at Quilt National '99.

Photo: Géard le Pioufle

The Gallery

**Le Cyclone Nine
(The Ninth Hurricane)**

26" x 26" (66 cm x 66 cm)

Odile wanted to interpret the very traditional nine-patch design, but instead of playing with the squares, she decided to play with the seams.

Photo: Gérard le Pioufle

Que la Lumière Soie
(Let There Be Light)

39" x 39" (99 cm x 99 cm)
Using silks from Lyon, Odile
tried to design $1/4$" lines that
look as straight as possible.

Photo: Gérard Le Pioufle

Maguelonne

65" x 50" (165 cm x 122 cm)
Imagine the light through a
stained-glass window.
Maguelonne is a cathedral close
to where Odile lives that no
longer has stained glass windows.

Photo: Géard Le Pioufle

Ainsi Soies Telles
(So Be It)

35" x 35" (89 cm x 89 cm)

This quilt is made with fabric from a Thai silk dress. For the first time, Odile dared to cut her fabrics free-hand without a rotary cutter.

Photo: Gérard Le Pioufle

Diptique I

37" x 35" (94 cm x 89 cm)

Study of light in warm and cool colors.

Photo: Gérard le Pioufle

Diptique II

37" x 35" (94 cm x 89 cm)

Study of light in warm and cool colors.

Photo: Gérard le Pioufle

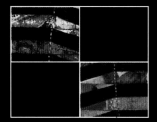
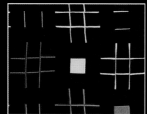
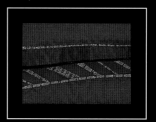

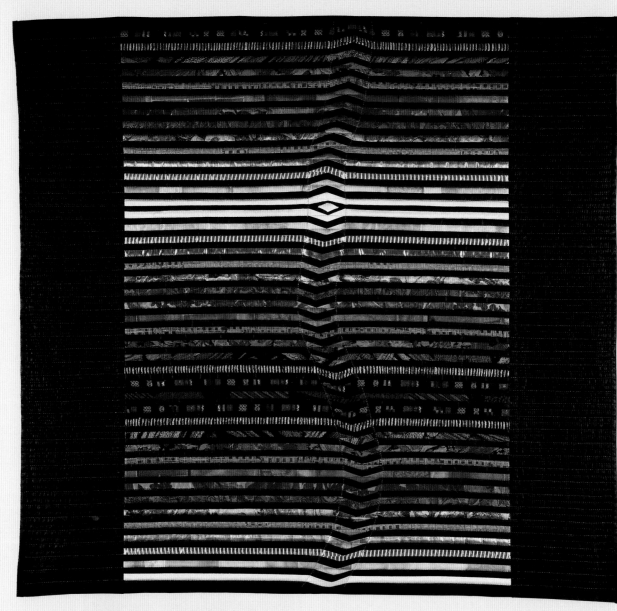

The Project

Traboules

33" x 36" (84 cm x 91 cm)

This quilt has been assembled by alternating colored strips with black ones using paper piecing.

Photo: Gérard Le Pioufle

Materials

Amounts are based on 45" (115 cm) fabric width.

■ 2³/₄ yards (2.5 m) of black fabric for the strips, border, backing, and binding

■ ¹/₄ yard (23 cm) each of fourteen different colored fabrics

■ 40" x 42" (104 cm x 107 cm) of black batting

■ Printing paper

Cutting

■ Forty-four ³/₄" x 45" (1.9 cm x 115 cm) strips of black fabric. Cut a 4" (10 cm) piece from each strip (small strips).

■ Six ³/₄" x 45" (1.9 cm x 115 cm) strips from each colored fabric. Cut a 4" (10 cm) piece from each strip.

■ Two 5" x 36" (12.7 cm x 91.5 cm) strips of black fabric for the side borders.

■ 40" x 42" (102 cm x 107 cm) for the backing.

■ Four 1¹/₂" x 45" (4 cm x 115 cm) strips for the binding.

Paper piecing method

■ The seams are represented by the drawn lines on the paper. Use a thin-point black felt-tipped pen to draw the lines.

■ Fabrics are secured on the right side of the paper.

■ Use a small stitch length. Your seams will be stronger and the paper will be easier to remove.

■ Position the first fabric right side up on the wrong side of the paper.

■ Position the subsequent fabrics wrong side up.

■ Sew on the lines with the paper on top.

Assembly

Notes:

■ *It is recommended that you make a sample before starting the project.*

■ *Alternate black and colored strips.*

■ *Instructions are given for a quilt design with the triangles lined up straight vertically. If you want the triangles of your quilt to form a curving line (as shown in the photograph) move the drawn dots on the lines accordingly. Be sure the dots are 4" (10 cm) apart.*

1. Use printing paper, either in rolls or large sheets. If your sheets are not large enough, you can tape two or three together to obtain the right size. The sheet of paper should measure 24" x 35" (61 cm x 89 cm). Draw your lines with a thin-point black felt-tipped pen so that you can see the lines on the wrong side of the paper. Draw all of the lines ¹/₂" (1.3 cm) apart on a piece of thin paper. You can use the pattern given on page 22, lengthening and adding lines as needed, or measure and draw your own. The borders will be added later without using the paper.

2. Draw a star in the center of one of the lines. On this same line, draw a dot 2" (5 cm) to the left of the star and another dot 2" (5 cm) to the right of the star. Repeat this process on all lines. The dots will show you where to put the 4" (10 cm) strip and the star will show you where to fold the strips into a triangle later in the process.

3. Starting with black in the middle, pin a long black strip of fabric onto the wrong side of the paper covering the two lines on the paper.

4. Place one small 4" black strip between the dots (right side down), on top of the long black strip. Before sewing, hold the paper up to the light to be sure the fabric piece covers the area and extends at least $1/4$" (6 mm) beyond the stitching line. Stitch along the top sewing line. Press.

5. Repeat step 4 to add a second small strip, but stitch along the bottom sewing line. Press.

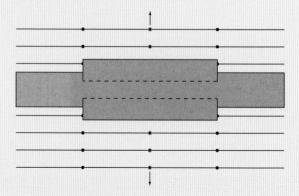

Stitch small black strips on the wrong side of the paper, and press open.

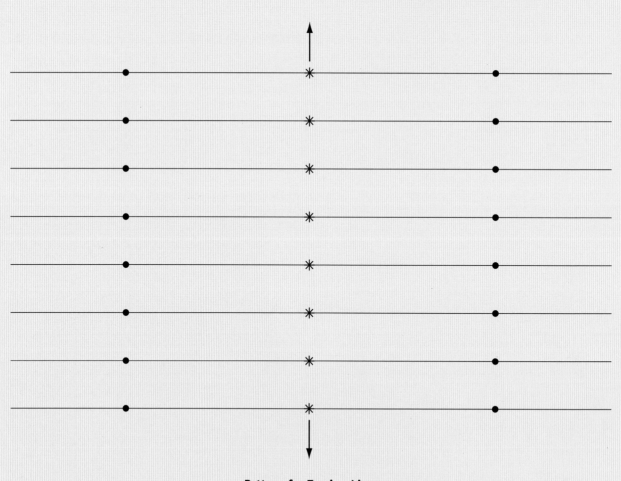

Pattern for Tracing Lines

6. Using two long strips of one color, sew the left strip wrong side up, starting at the edge of the small strip with a small back stitch. Stitch to the edge of the paper. Press open.

7. Sew the right strip the same way. Do not catch the left strip in the stitches. Press seams open.

8. With a pencil, mark the top of the formed triangle (*) on the black fabric.

9. Fold the colored strips, making them intersect exactly on the pencil mark and pin them together.

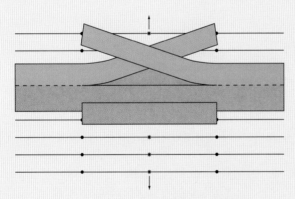

Fold strips to intersect at mark.

10. Sew a small strip of one color between the dots, wrong side up. Trim off long colored strips. Press the seams open.

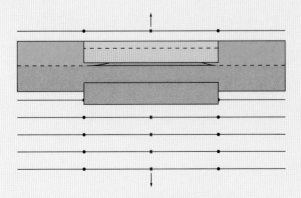

Placement of small colored strip.

11. Sew two long black strips (as in steps 6 and 7).

12. Fold, secure, and sew as you did previously.

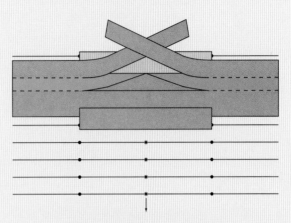

Fold strips to intersect at mark.

Important:

■ *Don't forget to alternate the colored and black strips as you go.*

13. When you have added strips to half of the paper, rotate the paper and repeat the process, adding strips to the other half. A diamond will appear in the center of the quilt top.

14. Final touch: Appliqué a small white diamond to the center.

Finishing

Layer and quilt with smoky-colored, monofilament thread on each side of the triangles. Extend the quilting on the black borders, but alternate one line of smoky invisible thread and one of multicolor metallic thread. Quilt vertically on each side of the triangles, with the same metallic thread. Bind.

ANNE
WORINGER

Anne Woringer was born in Paris and started sewing at a very early age. She is fascinated by the diversity of fabrics and enjoys discovering the creativity and background influence of many artists. She has adapted all

The Artist

that knowledge to her own work. ■ Anne's personal search into contemporary quilts began with Michael James' seminars—a revelation; the infinite world of contemporary quilts. ■ More recently she decided to start dyeing her own fabrics. She likes to use old linens that she finds at antique shops. Each time she experiments with her dyeing process, she discovers new shades and tones. She loves creating contemporary quilts using these fabrics, which already have their own story. ■ Her fabrics are not assembled in a traditional way. She puts many layers on top of each other and sews them with noticeable machine stitches—like the saddle stitch on leather. In fact, after being dyed, these old linens look more like buckskin. She works with dark deep colors, similar to those in Amish quilts. ■ Anne's popular lectures explain the wonderful creativity involved in contemporary quilts. Quilters and non-quilters love to attend her lectures and admire the visual accompaniments she provides.

Quetzalcoatl

42" x 42" (107 cm x 107 cm) Personal interpretation of a crazy quilt, made with the strip piecing method. Accepted at Quilt National in 1993.

Photo: Bruno Jarret

The Gallery

Claustra IV (Rumeur)

58" x 58" (147 cm x 147 cm)

This quilt is based on a free interpretation of Log Cabin construction.

Photo: Bruno Jarret

Aurore (Dawn)

48" x 51" (122 cm x 130 cm)
This is the first quilt made with
her own dyed fabrics. Her silk,
linen, and cotton fabrics have
all been dyed in only one
color—gold.

It's interesting to see how
the different fabrics react to
the same dye. Exhibited at
World Quilt in Japan in 1998
organized by Nihon Vogue.

Photo: Bruno Jarret

Chairs I

37" x 42" (94 cm x 107 cm)
This quilt, which is part of a large
series of "Chairs" quilts, can be
categorized as architectural. This
is the first time Anne hand dyed
19th-century linen fabrics.

Photo: Bruno Jarret

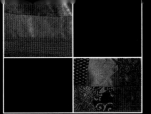

The Project

Nocturne (Nocturnal)

47" x 50" (119 cm x 127 cm)
Made using hand-dyed vintage linens, silk, and solid cotton fabrics.

This quilt has been assembled with a personal curve method that Anne has used and perfected.

Photo: Bruno Jarret

he technique itself is quite simple. The overall effect will depend on the variety, colors, and textures of the fabrics. This kind of quilt's uniqueness depends on the way the stratas will be sewn together. Nothing can really be planned in advance; this will be a combination of pure chance and selection of fabrics and colors.

Materials

Amounts are based on a 45" (115 cm) fabric width.

■ A large variety of coordinated fabrics—solids and prints from the same tone

■ Some contrasting fabrics which have visual unity—complementary subdued colors, warm/cool etc.

■ 3 yards (2.7 m) for backing

■ 53" x 56" (135 cm x 142 cm) of batting

■ ¹/₂ yard (46 cm) for binding (optional)

Cutting

With a rotary cutter and ruler, cut strips in various widths avoiding parallelism. While cutting these strips, try to imagine the final effect they will produce once they are sewn together.

Assembly

Use a ¹/₄" (6 mm) seam allowance.

1. Assemble the strips randomly until you achieve a 47" (119 cm) or wider width (stratum). Take color harmony into consideration, but also follow your instincts and inspiration.

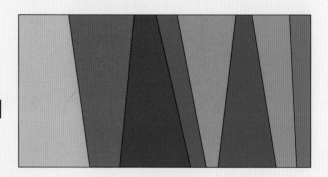

Stratum

2. Create as many strata as you desire. Each one should be different.

3. For cotton fabrics, press the seams toward the darkest fabric whenever possible. If you use different thicknesses of fabrics, press the seams toward the thinnest fabrics. If all your fabrics are quite thick, press the seams open.

4. Select one stratum. Make a softly-curved cut from one edge of the stratum to the other approximately 2¹/₂"-3" (6.4 cm-7.6 cm) from the straight bottom edge of the stratum.

5. Make a second softly curved cut 2¹/₂"-3" (6.4 cm-7.6 cm) from the first curved cut.

Cut two soft curves.

6. Lay this curved stratum strip next to another stratum or fabric piece, moving it laterally until you like the look. The strips in each stratum should not match each other, but the colors should be coordinated or complementary.

7. Occassionally insert a solid or printed strip of fabric.

8. Place your stratum or fabric piece ¹/₄" (6 mm) under the curved stratum and cut using the first curve as a pattern.

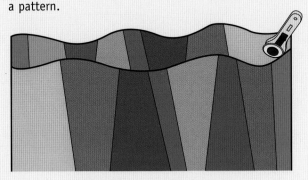

Place stratum or fabric under the curved stratum strip and cut.

9. Pin carefully and sew each curve using a ¹/₄" (6 mm) seam allowance. This is a very simple assembling method because the curves are soft. If you decide to make deeper curves, you should use a template just as in any traditional curved block, such as Drunkards Path or Double Wedding Ring.

10. Repeat steps 5–9, adding curved strips until your piece measures approximately 50" (127cm).

Finishing

1. In Nocturne, Anne has hand quilted in the ditch all the thin fabrics (such as silk or thin cotton), as those fabrics tend not to be completely flat when sewn next to thicker ones. The quilting helps make the fabrics lay flat.

2. Cut the quilt into a circle, rectangle, or square, and finish with or without binding.

RUTH EISSFELDT

Ruth Eissfeldt discovered patchwork after seeing an antique quilt exhibition in Düsseldorf in the 1970s. The graphic effect of these quilts fascinated her. ■ Innovation, even if it is inspired by something else, touches her more than any other aspect of contemporary quiltmaking. She admires different styles of architecture, particularly the variety of houses, churches, and castles that exist in Europe. ■ Her designs are made with large pieces of fabric. In order to give more space to the fabrics, she proceeds as though making a collage, mixing different textures and using new and antique fabrics from any origin. ■ Ruth likes to use a variety of fabrics: cotton, silk, velvet, brocade—whatever inspires her and stimulates her creativity. She collects fabrics for many years before starting a project. Together, the fabrics, their structure, and their colors inspire her and she never loses this feeling during the creation of her new project. The print of the fabrics can be abstract, floral, striped, or geometrical. ■ The quilting is very important for Ruth; it is another way to add dimension to her work. All of her quilts are machine quilted. Ruth believes that machine quilting shouldn't imitate hand quilting—it is a technique in itself.

The Artist

Messing
39" x 41" (98 cm x 105 cm)
This is a small quilt Ruth made after finishing *Gold (on page 32)*. *Messing*'s design is much stricter than *Gold*'s. It could represent a ground plan of a Japanese garden. This quilt was exhibited in Tokyo in 1998 and won the bronze award.

Photo: Peter Braatz

Kleine Grüne Wolke (Little Green Cloud)

54" x 52" (137 cm x 132 cm)

Ruth was inspired by Heide Stoll-Weber's hand-dyed fabrics. She calls the value differences "Farbfelder" (Color Fields).

Photo: Peter Braatz

The Gallery

Grau (Gray)

52" x 62" (132 cm x 158 cm)

Gray is a noble color—the color of distinction. In this quilt, Ruth mixed different types of fabrics, using fabrics for evening dresses as well as fabrics for men's suits, wool, silk, cotton, and viscose. The only connection between all these textiles is the color gray.

Photo: Peter Braatz

Gold

49" x 53" (125 cm x 135 cm)

This quilt belongs to a series of
black/gold and black/silver quilts.
They are also meditative quilts.

Photo: Peter Braatz

Swan II

52" x 47" (132 cm x 119 cm)
A few years ago Ruth saw a film
called *A Love of Swann,* which
was based on Marcel Proust's
book *In Search of Lost Time.*
All the actors were dressed in
white, and she couldn't forget
the wonderful impression this
film left with her. She then
made three quilts thinking about
that film: *Swan I, Swan II,* and
A Love of Swan, (deliberately
removing the second "n" from
Swann's name).

Photo: Peter Braatz

Purpur (Purple)

53" x 55" (135 cm x 140 cm)
Purple-red is the color of kings'
and emperors' robes, as well as
those of high-ranking members
of the Christian church. In the
past, it was a very precious color
for fabric, and ordinary people
were not allowed to use it. Ruth
collected these fabrics for a long
time before starting to make
this quilt.

Photo: Peter Braatz

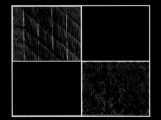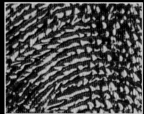

The Project

Rustan

36" x 38" (91 cm x 96 cm)

Rustan belongs to a series of thirteen quilts called "The Persian Letters" (Die persischen Briefe) after Montesquieu's first book (from the 18th century.)

This book is mainly a fictitious correspondence between a distinguished Persian and his friends. Rustan is the name of one of his true friends, with whom he discusses his absence from Persia.

Photo: Peter Braatz

ustan is the first quilt Ruth made without a traditional block construction. It is a free composition.

Amounts are based on 45" (115 cm) fabric width.

■ A variety of fabrics: cotton, silk, velvet, brocade—whatever inspires you—for the quilt top

■ 1 ¼ yards (1.1 m) of solid-colored cotton fabric for backing

■ 42" x 44" (107 cm x 112 cm) of thin cotton batting

■ ¼ yard (23 cm) for binding

Cutting

You can cut your fabrics to the exact size shown on the diagram or work spontaneously, as Ruth does, without any previous planning. If you prefer to follow Ruth's construction: Rotary cut strips 4" (10.2 cm), 6" (15.2 cm), 8" (20.3 cm), 10" (25.4 cm), and 12" (30.5 cm) wide. Then cut these strips into rectangles or squares.

All measurements are in inches.

All measurements are in centimeters.

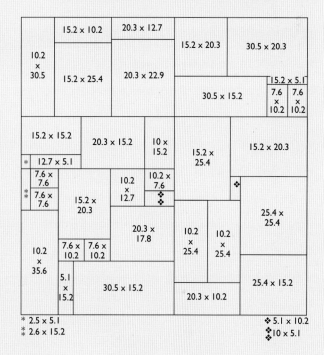

Quilt Diagrams

Design

You can place your rectangles and squares on a design wall, working intuitively and trying different fabrics and colors until you are satisfied with the composition, or follow the instructions below. Begin by placing the most striking fabric on the design wall. In *Rustan*, it is the blue-and-brown striped fabric in the left upper quarter. Place a gold fabric on one side and an interesting golden black on the left, overlapping the fabrics slightly. Next, place all the blue brocade.

Assembly

Use a $1/4$" (6 mm) seam allowance.

1. If some of the thin fabrics need more body, iron some cotton viseline or lightweight interfacing to the back of the fabric pieces. Then return the pieces to the design wall. This will be done on each shape individually.

2. Work in units of four. Place the first two pieces with right sides together and stitch, then place the next two adjacent fabrics with right sides together and stitch. Press the seams open and trim each unit to match the one next to it.

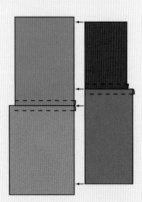

Work in units of four.

3. Place each unit back on the design wall. If you cannot work in units of four, assemble the odd pieces first, stopping $1/4$" (6 mm) before the end of the seam, if necessary, to fit the next piece in. This technique will enable you to keep track of which pieces go where.

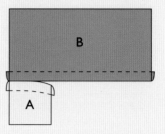

Stop stitching $1/4$" (6 mm) from the end.

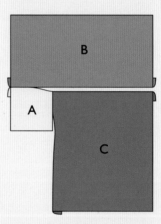

Stitch the next piece. Stop stitching $1/4$" (6 mm) from the end.

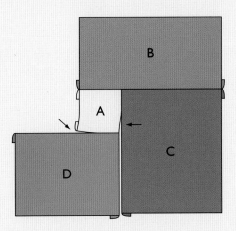

Stitch the next piece.

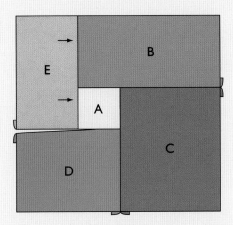

Continue adding pieces.

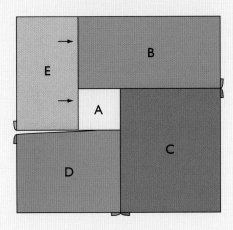

Finished Section

1. Layer the quilt and baste carefully every 6" (15 cm) to obtain a nice flat quilt.

2. Because of all the different seams and thicknesses of the fabrics, the quilting is easier by machine. Quilt using a very simple zigzag pattern that changes direction, matching the vertical or horizontal pieces. To do this, first mentally divide the quilt top in half and quilt the first zigzag line across the whole quilt. Quilt 1" (2.5 cm) from the first line all the way down the first half, and then again from the middle outwards for the second half.

Quilting Pattern

3. Once the quilting is complete, trim the four sides of the quilt even and bind with a thin strip of various fabrics matching the quilt.

DORLE STERN-STRAETER

While living in the United States, **Dorle Stern-Straeter** became interested in quilting and attended classes with some of the great American quilt designers. ■ After a move to Saudi Arabia—with its desert and highly modern architecture—she was inspired to such an extent

The Artist

that she gradually changed her style and techniques from curves to the crazy patchwork technique. Out of necessity, as there were no fabric shops, every tiny scrap of fabric she brought with her was used in her work. ■ Dorle later returned to Germany, where she continues to perfect her crazy patchwork technique. Her compositions are very structured and organized around repeated blocks that are always assembled with templates. She systematically plays with geometrical forms, colors, and gradations—everything is carefully planned. The strict structure of her quilts contrasts with her freedom in using colors and fabrics. This contrast is the reason her quilts are so intriguing. ■ Dorle has tried to develop more creative and inspirational quilting among German quilters through lectures and workshops which she gives around her own country and throughout Europe. She has been invited to exhibit her work all over the world and has been accepted at Quilt National and Visions.

Trio I

58" x 72" (147 cm x 183 cm)
Three long red bars in the middle of the quilt sit on a black background. Tiny multicolored triangles seem to dance in front of the quilt.

Photo: Patricia Fliegauf

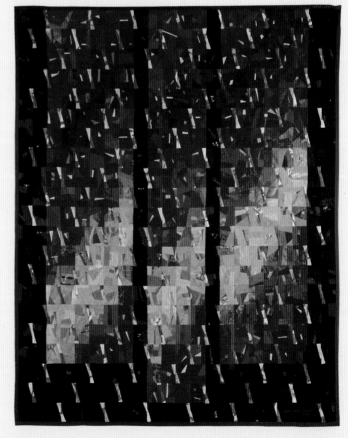

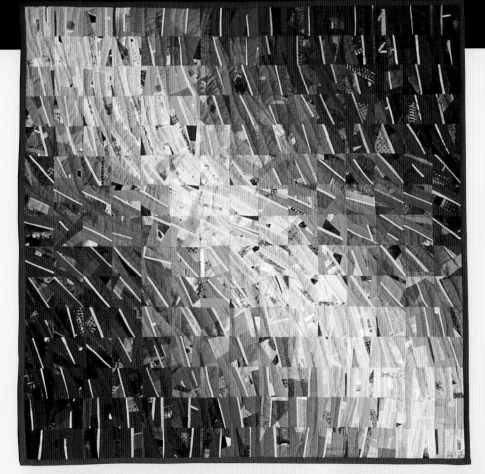

Reflection

47" x 47" (119 cm x 119 cm)
This quilt was made using the crazy patchwork technique with a square. Long, narrow, contrasting pieces and the color gradation give direction and movement to this quilt.

Photo: Patricia Fliegauf

Aquarium

56" x 56" (142 cm x 142 cm)
This is a quilt with visual movement.

By narrowing the blocks, Dorle obtains the illusion of curvature in lines without curves.

Photo: Patricia Fliegauf

Graffitti IV

60" x 55" (152 cm x 140 cm)
Dorle was inspired by hand-written pieces of silk. Large pieces of silk in cool and warm colors are pieced to a black background.

Photo: Patricia Fliegauf

The Gallery

Im Schilf (In the Rushes)

55" x 60" (140 cm x 152 cm)

This quilt was inspired by the

landscape in the north of Germany.

Photo: Patricia Fliegauf

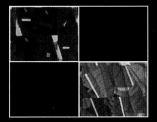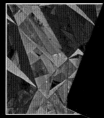

The Project

Marimekko I

47" x 50" (119 cm x 117 cm)

Dorle was inspired by the multi-color, multi-design fabrics made in Finland and, using her wave-crazy piecing technique, she created this very interesting quilt.

Photo: Patricia Fliegauf

Materials

Amounts are based on 45" (115 cm) fabric width.

■ 2 yards (1.8 m) of Marimekko print or similar fabric (with different shades on the same piece) or a wide range of assorted fabrics — 1/4 yard (23 cm) each of a minimum of eight fabrics

■ Strips and scraps from light to dark (here, turquoise to dark blue), matching your printed fabric for the crazy patchwork technique

■ Small strips of a contrasting color (here, orange)

■ 3 yards (2.7 m) for backing

■ 53" x 56" (135 cm x 142 cm) of batting

■ 1/2 yard (46 cm) for binding

■ Template plastic

Cutting

■ It is difficult to give the exact number of strips to be cut or the number of fabrics to be used. Dorle never cuts her strips in advance — she improvises as she goes along.

■ The crazy patchwork pieces can only be constructed by sewing some fabrics together randomly.

■ Your strips may be from 1 1/4" to 3" (3.2 cm to 7.6 cm) wide or more. Sometimes you might want to emphasize the print of the fabric; other times you might want to use strips in a small amount just as an accent. The width of your strips will be cut accordingly.

Assembly

Use a 1/4" (6mm) seam allowance. You will use the **crazy patchwork and the wave techniques.**

Crazy Patchwork Technique

1. Start sewing two turquoise strips together. Press, then cut diagonally into smaller pieces.

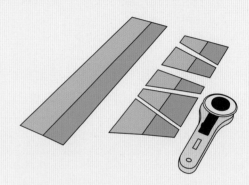

Sew strips, press, and cut diagonally.

2. Sew two other strips together and add the small pieces you just cut, matching their bias side to the straight grain of the strip. Press toward the strip.

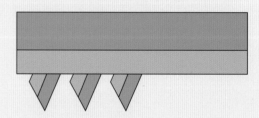

Sew two strips together and add the small pieces.

3. Free-cut following the diagonal lines.

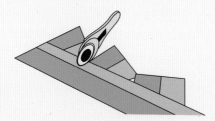

Free-cut following the diagonal lines.

4. Sew the newly cut pieces to a new strip of fabric. Remember to always sew the bias side of the new shapes to the straight grain of the strip. Once in a while, add a small strip of orange or any other contrasting fabric.

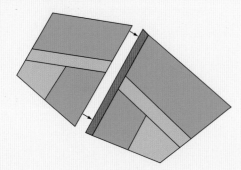

Sew the newly counter-cut pieces to a new strip of fabric.

5. Continue sewing in the same way until you have assembled a sufficiently large piece to cut a rectangle measuring 7" x 5^1/$_2$" (17.8 cm x 14 cm). The orange accent strip should be in the middle, perpendicular to what will be your wave cut edge.

Wave Technique

1. Cut one 7" x 5^1/$_2$" (17.8 cm x 14 cm) rectangle from the Marimekko fabric and one rectangle from the crazy piece.

2. Stack the rectangles both right side up on top of each other. Place the crazy patchwork rectangle on top to have more control while you cut. Cut three waves in your rectangles.

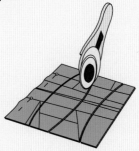

Lay rectangles right side up on top of each other. Cut three waves.

3. Place the cut rectangles side by side.

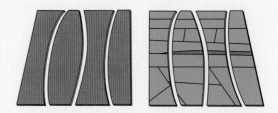

Place the cut rectangles side by side.

4. Alternating a solid piece with a crazy patchwork piece, lay the pieces on a piece of paper, so you can easily move your work to your sewing machine without confusion. Each rectangle will have two solid pieces of fabric and two pieces with the crazy patchwork technique.

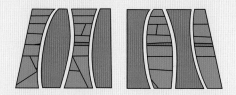

Alternate the solid fabric pieces with the crazy patchwork pieces.

5. Sew the pieces together, matching the edges. Press away from the crazy patchwork background or toward the darkest fabric when possible. Repeat for all blocks.

6. Place one block so the seams are horizontal. Using the trapezoid Template 1 (page 45), trim the block. Repeat for *all of the interior* blocks. You can vary the length of the trapezoid by trimming three sides, sliding the template to form a more elongated trapezoid, and trimming the fourth side.

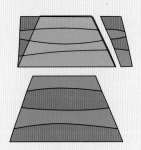

Trim.

7. Arrange your blocks on the design wall.

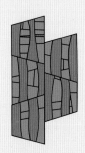

Arrange the blocks.

8. Cut the remaining top and bottom edge and corner blocks with the trapezoid Template 2 (page 45) that has 90° angles, placing the 90° angles in the appropriate corners.

9. Once your blocks are arranged, sew them together vertically following the diagram. Trim to square up quilt top.

Quilt Assembly

Finishing

1. The design of the quilt is strong enough that it should not be disturbed with a quilting pattern — quilt in the ditch of the wave pieces only.

2. Once the quilting is complete, trim the sides even and bind your quilt with a narrow strip of any matching fabric.

Template 1

Template 2

90°

HEIDE STOLL-WEBER

In 1986 **Heide Stoll-Weber** bought a new sewing machine to make clothes. Instead of clothing, she made her first quilt and was immediately hooked. Everything fell into place: composition, geometry, and her love for color, fabric, and sewing. She bought books and taught herself new techniques. ■ Quilt Expo Europa in Salzburg in 1988 gave her a chance to see hundreds of quilts which used different techniques and designs. She gave the quilts undivided attention. Everything was new and interesting, and technical details were unsolvable mysteries. ■

The Artist

In the 1980s there were not many chances to attend quilting workshops with international teachers in Germany, but Heide attended classes whenever she had the opportunity. ■ In 1990 Heide took a class from Nancy Crow. Nancy became her strongest influence and her mentor. Nancy gave her the improvisational techniques that enabled her to work spontaneously and achieve what she always wanted: painting with fabrics and sewing-machine stitches. ■ Heide sells her hand-dyed fabrics and teaches fabric dyeing, patchwork, and color theory throughout Europe and in the United States. Her work has been accepted into numerous international exhibits.

Entrance
12" x 16" (30 cm x 40 cm)
Small intuitive work, which reflects Heide's emotional states.
Photo: Helmut Fricke

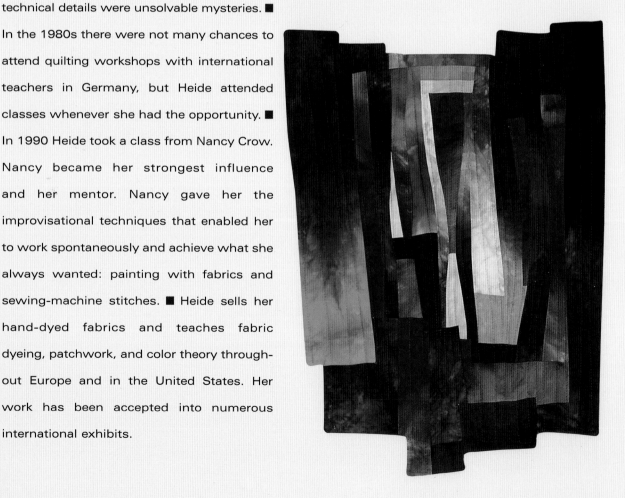

The Gallery

Sunset

16" x 24" (41 cm x 61 cm)

Constantly changing clouds and skies
were the inspiration for this quilt.

Photo: Helmut Fricke

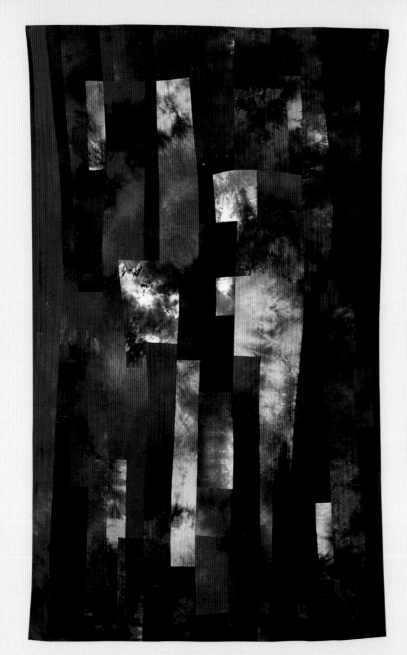

Fairy Castle

12" x 16" (30 cm x 40 cm)

In this quilt, Heide decided
to combine nature with
architecture.

Photo: Helmut Fricke

Glow

45" x 80" (114 cm x 200 cm)

Heide let the fabrics inspire her
when creating this quilt.

Photo: Helmut Fricke

Relief

72" x 56" (183 cm x 142 cm)

This quilt received the Award of Merit at Quilt National 1999.

Photo: Helmut Fricke

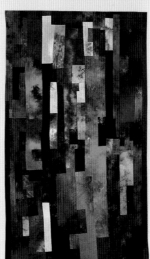

Reef

46" x 80" (115 cm x 200 cm)

Heide decided to challenge herself by introducing a pastel pink fabric (she hates that color) into this quilt and making the best of it.

Photo: Helmut Fricke

Windows to Paradise

53" x 75" (135 cm x 191 cm)

This quilt was exhibited at Quilt National '99 and received a Juror's Award of Merit.

Photo: Helmut Fricke

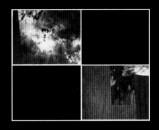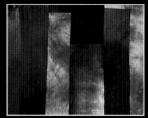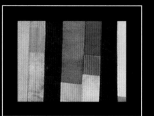

The Project

Falling Water

12" x 16" (31 cm x 41 cm)

Made especially for this book to explain Heide's techniques.

Photo: Helmut Fricke

Materials

■ A wide variety of fabric scraps with contrasting colors. Contrast may be dark/light, warm/cool, complementary, solid/textured, anything which appeals to you.

■ 20" x 26" (51 cm x 66 cm) for backing

■ 20" x 26" (51 cm x 66 cm) of batting

Cutting

The strips are cut freehand and placed on a design wall as you choose.

Assembly

Use a $^1/_4$" (6 mm) seam allowance.

1. Lay out a small composition of strips on a flannel-covered design wall so the fabric pieces stick to the flannel without pinning.

2. To sew a set in piece of fabric, position the piece to be set in face down on top of the fabric next to it on the design wall. Start $^1/_4$" (6 mm) from the upper edge with a few backstitches, then continue stitching to finish the first seam.

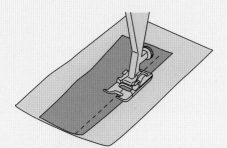

Stitch the first seam.

3. Trim the edge of the larger piece with small sharp scissors and stop cutting $^1/_2$" (12mm) from the upper edge of the smaller piece.

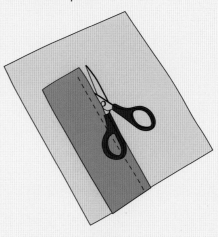

Trim.

4. Turn 90° to the right and cut to the edge of the fabric. Cut at a 45° angle where the seam starts.

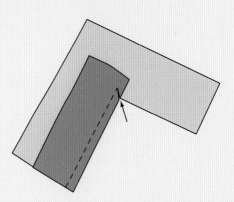

Cut a 45° angle.

5. Turn the fabric over to make a second seam towards the first one (stitch like a Y-seam). Stitch to the edge of the first seam.

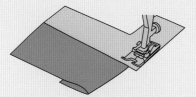

Stitch the second seam.

6. Press the set-in piece away from the other fabric.

7. Continue adding pieces following the design.

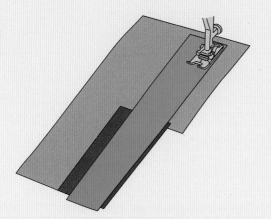

Continue adding pieces.

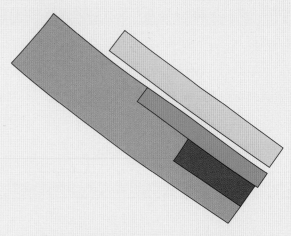

Cut through both layers to make the pieces fit together.

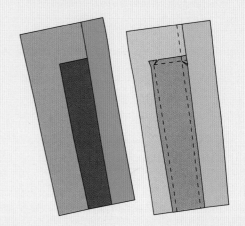

Front of Set-in Piece   **Back of Set-in Piece**

8. If you sew together freehand-cut pieces, place your fabrics side by side, overlapping slightly. Then cut through both layers. This will make both pieces fit together perfectly.

9. Sew one half of the design, then the other half, and assemble them together at the end. As you can see, there is a small variation from the original construction, but the overall view is unchanged.

Front

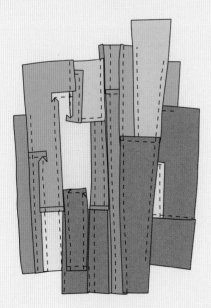

Back

1. Place the batting down first, with the backing, right side up, on top of it. Then place the quilt top, wrong side up, on top of the backing.

2. Sew along the edges of the quilt top, leaving about 15" (38 cm) unsewn, to turn the layers inside out like a pillowcase.

3. Trim the edges. Clip the corners.

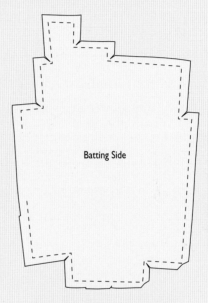

Batting Side

Sew, trim, and clip corners.

4. Turn the "pillowcase" right side out. Close the opening with a few hand stitches.

5. Machine quilt using monofilament thread in a continuous pattern.

ANCOBROUWERS-
BRANDERHORST

Anco Brouwers-Branderhorst has been teaching drawing and design with textiles for ten years. She enjoys every minute and every aspect of quilting. When she first started, she designed and planned the entire quilt

The Artist

first, including the fabric. Now her project grows as she goes and she rarely plans anything on paper. Her project evolves as she works, and she doesn't hesitate to change things as her quilt progresses. Even if she makes a drawing first, she does it in black and white, just to look at the contrasts, before playing with her fabrics. ■ She believes that the quilting is as important as the rest of the process. It enhances her work and supports the design or gives it a new direction. For Anco, the most important issue in her work is harmony and balance. ■ Anco pieces her quilts by machine and quilts by hand and machine. She never makes more than one or two quilts a year, since the hand quilting is so time consuming. In the meantime, she has plenty of new ideas she hopes to be able to put in practice. ■ Anco has exhibited her work at prestigious exhibitions in the Netherlands, United Kingdom, Denmark, and the United States.

Double
47" x 55" (120 cm x 140 cm)
The starting point of this quilt was a candle-light from Finland. The colors are also inspired by that country. First, the quilt was drawn in black, gray, and white; the colors were chosen later.
Photo: Anco Brouwers-Branderhorst

Northern Lights

62" x 70 (156 cm x 177 cm)
The design and colors of this quilt were inspired by the art, culture, and colors of the Scandinavian countries, which Anco loves and admires.

Photo: Anco Brouwers-Branderhorst

The Gallery

Material Thoughts

70" x 61" (178 cm x 155 cm)
This quilt shows a wide variety of forms, colors, materials, and textures. It even incorporates small pieces of wood! Harmony and balance, in both form and color, are very important in this quilt. By using pieces of wood, Anco wanted to create contrast in the structure and the appearance of the work.

Photo: Anco Brouwers-Branderhorst

Light

64" x 54" (162 cm x 136 cm)
In this quilt, the colors are placed so that it seems like the light shines in the dark.

Photo: Anco Brouwers-Branderhorst

Rolduc

49" x 44" (125 cm x 112 cm)
Anco got her inspiration for this quilt after attending a fabric dying workshop in Rolduc. Black zigzag paths are overlapping the hand-dyed fabric. The printed design is quilted over these paths. Quilted squares accentuate the design.

Photo: Anco Brouwers-Branderhorst

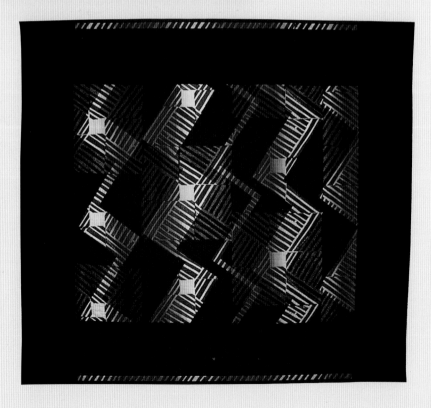

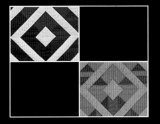  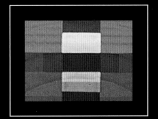 

The Project

Double Diagonal

63" x 71" (160 cm x 180 cm)

The design of this quilt is inspired by African textiles.

Anco likes to use simple shapes (strips, squares, and triangles), as in African designs. She played with the forms to create a new design.

Photo: Foto Dubach

he quilt is made using variations of one block. On three sides, the brown and gray strips continue into the border, sometimes crossing each other. The off-white strips of the blocks do not continue into the border, and are replaced by darker ones in order to enhance the blocks and give a new dimension to the borders.

Materials

Amounts are based on 45" (115 cm) fabric width.

- $^3/_4$ yard (70 cm) each of six different browns
- $^3/_4$ yard (70 cm) each of six different grays
- $1^1/_4$ yard (1 m) each of four different off-whites
- $^1/_8$ yard (12 cm) each of three different purples and three different blues
- 4 yards (3.7 m) for backing
- 78" x 70" (198 cm x 178 cm) of batting
- $^1/_2$ yard (46 cm) for binding
- 11" x $12^1/_4$" (27.9 cm x 31.1 cm) of template plastic

Block Construction

Cutting for Upper Left Half of Block

1. Cut forty-eight $1^1/_2$" (3 cm)-wide brown strips. Cut the strips into 9" strips (192 strips).

2. Cut forty-eight $1^1/_2$" (3 cm)-wide off-white strips. Cut the strips into 9" strips (192 strips).

3. Cut one $1^1/_2$" (3 cm)-wide strip from one purple fabric and two gray fabrics. Cut each strip into four 9" (23 cm) strips.

Assembly for Upper Left Half of Block

Use a $^1/_4$" (6 mm) seam allowance.

1. Sew eight dark brown and eight off-white 9" (23 cm) strips together, alternating brown, off-white, brown, off-white, etc. Press the seams in one direction.

2. Repeat to make twenty-four 9" x $16^1/_2$" (23 cm x 42 cm) rectangles, occasionally replacing a brown strip with a purple strip and an off-white strip with a gray strip.

Cutting for Lower Right Half of Block

1. Cut sixty $1^1/_2$" (3 cm)-wide gray strips.

Cut the strips into 17" strips (120 strips).

2. Cut sixty $1^1/_2$" (3 cm)-wide off-white strips.

Cut the strips into 17" strips (120 strips).

3. Cut one $1^1/_2$" (3 cm)-wide strip from each of

the three blue fabrics. Cut the strips into 17"

(43.2 cm) strips.

Assembly for Lower Right Half of Block

1. Sew five gray strips and five off-white 17" strips

together, alternating gray, off-white, gray, off-white,

etc. Press the seams in one direction.

2. Repeat to make twenty-four 17" x $10^1/_2$"

(43.2 cm x 26.7 cm) rectangles, occasionally replacing

an off-white strip with a blue strip.

Block Assembly

Finished block size: $12^1/_4$" x 11" (31.1 cm x 27.9 cm)

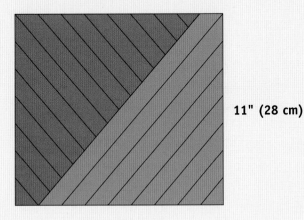

$12^1/_4$" (31.5 cm)

11" (28 cm)

1. Cut a piece of template plastic $12^3/_4$" x $11^1/_2$"

(32.4 cm x 29.2 cm). On one of the $11^1/_2$" (28 cm)

sides, mark a dot $1^5/_8$" (4 cm) from the top corner,

on the very edge of the plastic. Mark a dot $1^3/_8$"

(3.5 cm) from the first dot [still on the very edge of

the 11" (27.9 cm) side]. Continue marking dots $1^3/_8$"

(3.5 cm) apart all the way down the $11^1/_2$" (28 cm) side

(seven dots in all). The last dot should be $1^5/_8$"

(4 cm) from the bottom corner. Repeat for the other

$11^1/_2$" side. Write TOP on the top edge of the template.

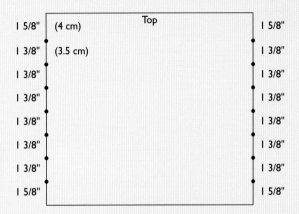

Block Template

2. Sew an Upper Left Half of Block rectangle to a

Lower Right Half of Block rectangle, orienting the

strips following the block assembly illustration.

3. Refer to the quilt photograph. Notice that the diagonal seam line that divides the block is not in the same place on each block. Position the template on your block, matching the dots with the seam lines. You have several options for placing the template. As long as you match the dots on the template with the seam lines on your block, the seam lines will match up when you stitch your blocks together. Trim the blocks using the template.

Seminole Sashing

Option 1: Using Leftover Strip Sets

1. If you want to use the leftover strip sets for the Seminole sashing, cut them into $1^{1}/2$" (3 cm) sections and separate them into three-strip units.

2. Follow steps 4 and 5 below. You will need five 49" (124.5 cm) sashing strips.

Option: 2: Using New Strips

1. Cut $1^{1}/2$" (3.8 cm) strips from fifteen fabrics.

2. Stitch three strips together into a strip set. Repeat for a total of seven strip sets.

3. Cut the strip sets into $1^{1}/2$" (3.8 cm) units.

4. Follow the illustration to position and stitch the units together. You will need five 49" sashing strips.

5. Trim following the illustration. Be sure to leave $1/4$" seam allowances.

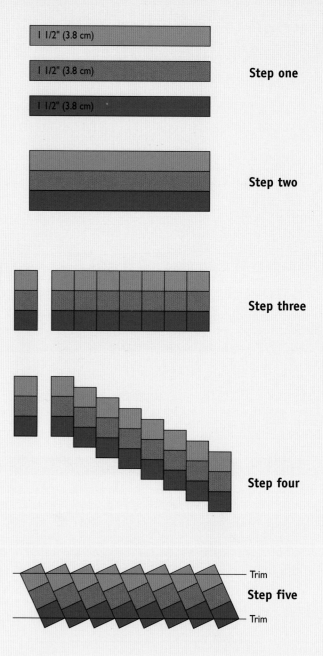

1 1/2" (3.8 cm)

1 1/2" (3.8 cm)

1 1/2" (3.8 cm)

Step one

Step two

Step three

Step four

Trim

Step five

Trim

Quilt Top Assembly

1. Stitch the blocks into rows. Press.

2. Add the sashing strips. Press.

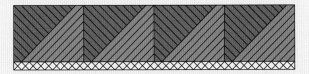

Add Sashing Strips.

3. Stitch the rows together. Press.

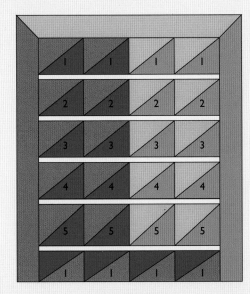

Quilt Diagram

Borders

1. Using leftover fabrics, piece together $1^1/2$" x 12" (3.8 cm x 30.5 cm) strips, staggering the strips $^3/4$" (1.9 cm) as in step Four for Seminole Sashing (page 60) so the strips can be at a 45° angle without too much waste. If you want the brown and gray strips to continue into the border as shown on the quilt photo, plan the border strips accordingly.

2. Measure the width and height of the quilt and piece the three other borders alternating the colors, lighter for the right border, darker for the left one, etc.

Borders

3. Optional: To obtain the basketweave effect for the lower left and lower right corners, cut the lower section of the border into $1^1/2$" (3 cm) units, place a $1^1/2$" (3 cm) strip between each pieced unit, and stitch the strips and units together. Trim the border to the correct length.

7. Add the borders to the quilt top.

Finishing

1. Layer and hand quilt in the ditch of all the off-white strips. With blue thread, quilt three lines per strip on the blue strips, continuing onto the off-white strips. In some parts, you may cross the lines to make square motifs.

2. Bind.

OLGA PRINS
LUKOWSKI

Olga Prins Lukowski was told that there is an artist inside everyone, although sometimes it is deeply hidden. The only thing to do is to let it come out. At the beginning, Olga didn't believe it, but she felt challenged and decided to explore her artistic side. ■ An old friend

The Artist

from school, who was a traditional quilter herself, convinced Olga that she should try patchwork and quilting. She was hooked and wanted to continue discovering the artist within herself. She later met Michael James, who gave her a big push to start working as an art-quilt maker. Olga uses the word "working" intentionally. She works five hours a day almost every day in her lovely studio. She not only makes quilts but also continuously studies designs through art books and visiting art exhibits. ■ Thanks to quilting, Olga has found a new balance in her life: during the day she works with her hands on her quilts and in her beautiful, immense garden; and at night she reads all kinds of books. ■ Olga is a very popular teacher in Europe and speaks at least four languages. She has exhibited her work all over the world and has been asked to judge many contests for prestigious art quilt exhibitions.

Da Vista (The Vista)
46" x 43" (115 cm x 110 cm)
An impression of the country of Olga's roots, Poland, with its large river, the Wisla. Cotton and silk.
Photo: Hennie J.C.M. Pardoel

The Gallery

De vier Elementen (The Four Elements)

42" x 45" (107 cm x 114 cm)

Cotton, silk, and mixed fabrics.

Photo: Hennie J.C.M. Pardoel

Mijn tuin in Vorjaar (My Garden in Spring)

38" x 38" (97 cm x 97)

Silks and upholstery fabrics.

Photo: Hennie J.C.M. Pardoel

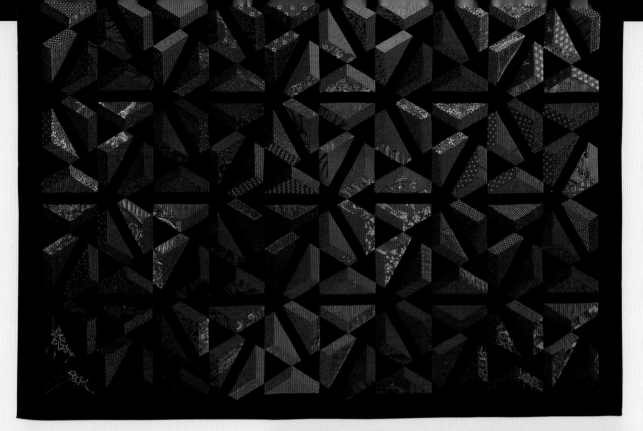

Het Vuur (The Fire)

53" x 35" (135 cm x 90 cm)

Cotton, silk, and polyester fabrics.

Photo: Hennie J.C.M. Pardoel

**Gekleurde Gevoelens
(Colored Feelings)**

39" x 39" (100 cm x 100 cm)

Cotton, silk, and polyester fabrics.

Photo: Hennie J.C.M. Pardoel

**De Graal
(The Holy Grail)**

35" x 43" (90 cm x 110 cm)
The Holy Grail, the goblet of
mystic power from the land of
the Druids, King Arthur, and the
Round Table. Cotton, silk, and
mixed fabrics.

Photo: Hennie J.C.M. Pardoel

**Mijn tuin in de
Herbst (My Garden
in Autumn)**

37" x 37" (95 cm x 95 cm)
Hand-dyed silk fabrics.

Photo: Hennie J.C.M. Pardoel

The Project

Bloemen Marlies
(Flowers for Marlies)

39" x 39" (100 cm x 100 cm).

Quilt made of silk fabrics using

Olga's foundation piecing method.

Photo: Hennie J.C.M. Pardoel

lga was unhappy with the traditional way of making crazy patchwork blocks, so she started experimenting with black paper squares. After much trial and error, she perfected the method that she uses in constructing her quilts.

Materials

Amounts are based on 45" (115 cm) fabric width.

■ A large number of scraps in bright colors for the flowers and various greens for the leaves.

■ 1¼ yards (1.2 m) of gray fabric for background, border, and binding. *Cut two 3¹/₂" x 45" strips of gray and two of black for the borders and two strips of gray and two of black for the binding, before cutting pieces for foundation piecing.*

■ 1¼ yards (1.2 m) of black fabric for background, border, and binding

■ 1¼ yards (1.2 m) for backing

■ 46" x 46" (112 cm x 112 cm) of batting

■ Three 5" x 5" (12.7 cm x 12.7 cm) pieces of paper; one black and two white

■ Foundation paper (lightweight, see-through paper)

Foundation Piecing Method

Flowers for Marlies **is made with sixteen 8" (20 cm) blocks.**

To avoid monotony, Olga played with the blocks using mirror imaging or turning them around. Each of these blocks has thirty-one pieces, but the number of pieces in each block can vary.

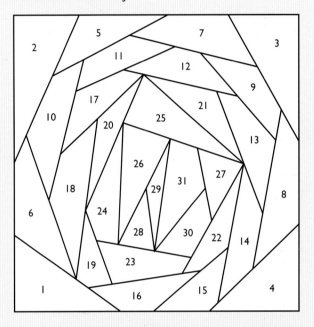

Block

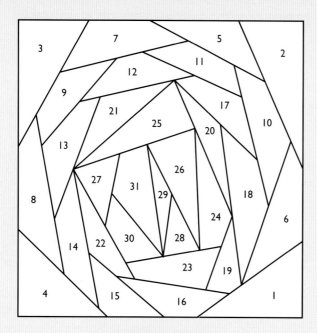

Mirror Image Block

Olga assembles all of her quilts using this method. She numbers her pieces from the outside to the center and starts sewing with the highest number (unlike most paper piecing methods which begin with #1). To learn the technique before starting a large project, Olga strongly recommends that you experiment with practice blocks.

1. Cut three 5" x 5" (12.7 cm x 12.7 cm) pieces of paper; one black and two white.

2. Cut a shape from the black square and number it "1". Draw that shape on one white square and label it with the number "1". Draw the same shape on the other white paper, but this time position it as the mirror image.

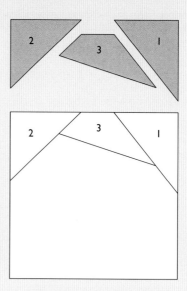

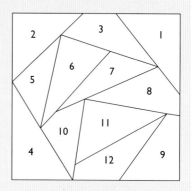

Cut and draw shapes.

Basic Design

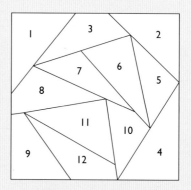

Basic Design Mirror Image

3. Cut another piece of black and number it "2". Draw it on the two white squares.

4. Continue until your entire black square is cut into pieces and drawn onto the white squares with the corresponding numbers.

5. This is your basic design and will allow you to follow your original design.

6. Use colored pencils to color on the basic design copies. Make two different compositions by reversing the placement of the dark and light on the two squares.

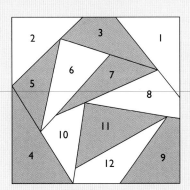

Block

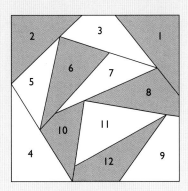

Block with Color Reversed

7. Make photocopies of your compositions, including the basic design. You may also mirror-image the blocks and photocopy them.

8. Start playing with the blocks.

9. Trace the blocks on foundation paper.

10. Starting with the highest numbered shape, place the first fabric right side up on the right side of the paper without the drawn lines, holding it up to the light so the drawn lines show through. Be sure the fabric piece extends at least $1/4$" beyond all sides of the shape.

11. Place the second fabric right side down on top of it with the edge of the fabric extending at least $1/4$" into the next highest numbered shape. Sew on the drawn line of the foundation paper. When you press the fabric piece open, it will completely cover the next highest numbered shape. Continue as in step 10 for the next highest numbered shape and for all remaining shapes.

12. Attach the borders.

Finishing

1. Layer and quilt by hand or machine.

2. Attach a narrow binding matching the border fabrics.

CHARLOTTE YDE

Charlotte Yde of Denmark saw her first quilt at the age of sixteen while visiting relatives in Connecticut. She was touring the countryside with her uncle when she saw a quilt in a dark corner of a humble barn sale. She

The Artist

knows now that it was a traditional Double Wedding Ring, probably from the 1920s, but at the time she knew absolutely nothing about quilts and could not identify it.

She was fascinated by what could be done with fabrics, combining colors and changing the texture with quilting. Unfortunately, she couldn't afford to buy that quilt. ■ Later, Charlotte studied art history, but she knew that what she really wanted was to concentrate on non-traditional quiltmaking. She has always been attracted to the relief effect of quilting and loves playing with colors and shapes. ■ The process of making quilts has enriched her life in many ways. The struggles and the rewarding moments are what make her repeat the experience over and over again. There are always new challenges. ■ Teaching throughout Europe, exhibiting all over the world, and, most of all, being a member of Quilt Art New Work, is a joy and pleasure, since there are few Danish quilt artists. Belonging to that group makes her feel less isolated.

Polluted Thoughts

47" x 53" (120 cm x 135 cm)
Machine pieced and quilted.
The African batik fabrics reminded Charlotte of ribs and lungs, while some hand-dyed gray fabrics looked like pollution and dirt. However, her most sinister thoughts were belied by the quite pleasant color scheme of the finished quilt.

Photo: Dennis Rosenfeldt

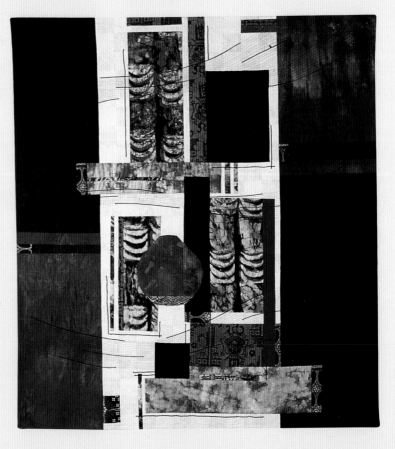

Green Irish Forest Quilt #1

43" x 59" (110 cm x 150 cm) Hand-dyed and commercial cotton and cotton sateen. Machine pieced and hand quilted. After fourteen days in Annaghmakerrig, Ireland, Charlotte made a couple of quilts in which she tried to reproduce the greenery of the Irish landscape and portray the wet forests surrounding the Tyrone Guthrie Center where she was staying.

Photo: Dennis Rosenfeldt

The Gallery

Ritual Signs

51" x 65" (130 cm x 165 cm) Machine pieced, hand appliquéd, and hand quilted. This quilt has signs and motifs from many different cultures and ages.

It includes Japanese ikat, Indonesian batik, the silhouette of a Danish knife for the Stone Age, and quilted patterns from old Danish rock carvings.

Photo: Dennis Rosenfeldt

**Metaphor—
Sunrise**

48" x 56" (121 cm x 143 cm)

**Metaphor—
Sea and Sky**

42" x 55" (106 cm x 140 cm)

Both above photos:

Hand-dyed cotton sateen.
Machine pieced and quilted. Hand
embroidered. Part of a series that
deals with color, depth, and emotion.
By breaking the rectangular format,
Charlotte tried to emphasize the
feeling of depth. In *Sunrise,* she
contradicts the inherent spatial
qualities of the colors.

Photo: Dennis Rosenfeldt

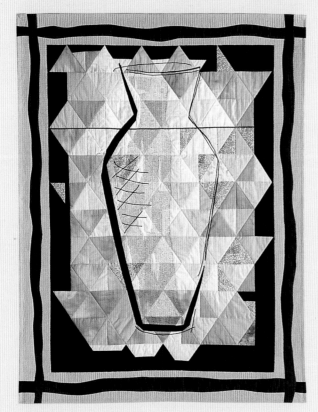

Red Horizon Line

45" x 59" (115 cm x 150 cm)
Machine pieced and quilted.
Vases and jars have been a
recurrent motif in Charlotte's
quilts for many years. The
shadow on the left side of the
vase is machine quilted with
hand spun black thread.

Photo: Dennis Rosenfeldt

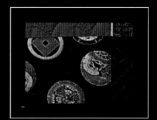

The Project

Japanese Impressions II

52" x 49" (132 cm x 125 cm) Machine pieced, machine and hand quilted. Old Japanese silk fabrics mixed with modern commercial fabrics. Charlotte created her own Japanese image.

Photo: Dennis Rosenfeldt

harlotte's inspiration for Japanese Impressions II *came from a book showing pictures of entrances to Japanese houses. This quilt was not planned; it grew on the wall step-by-step. Her fabrics guided the construction of the quilt.*

Materials

Amounts are based on 45" (115 cm) fabric width.

■ Any kind of fabrics; silk, cotton, or hand-dyed fabrics for the quilt top and binding. It is important to maintain a balance between all of the fabrics.

■ Contrasting colors for flat piping

■ 3 yards (2.7 m) for backing

■ 55" x 57" (140 cm x 145 cm) of batting

■ $^3/_8$ yard (30 cm) for binding

Cutting

Cut rectangles, strips, and squares, referring to the illustration on page 75 and the photograph.

Assembly

Use a $^1/_4$" (6mm) seam allowance.

1. Place the pieces on a design wall. The most important thing is to achieve balance between the fabrics and the colors.

2. Assemble in sections. To outline some of the fabrics, sew flat piping between the shapes. This will give more dimension to the whole quilt.

Finishing

1. Hand quilt, varying the quilting designs to give a new texture to the fabrics. Use Japanese quilting designs on some sections.

2. Bind using some of the fabrics from the quilt.

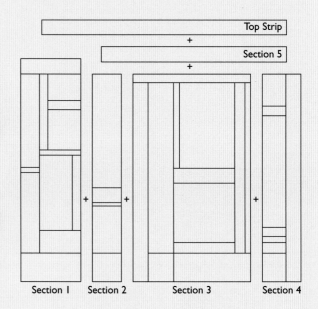

Quilt Assembly

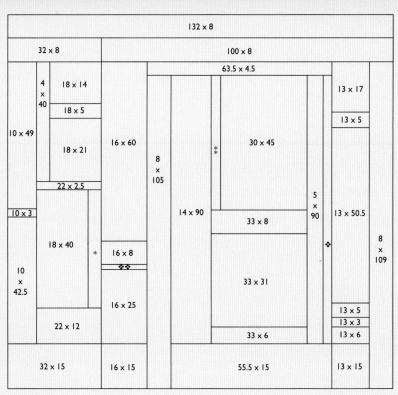

All measurements are in centimeters.

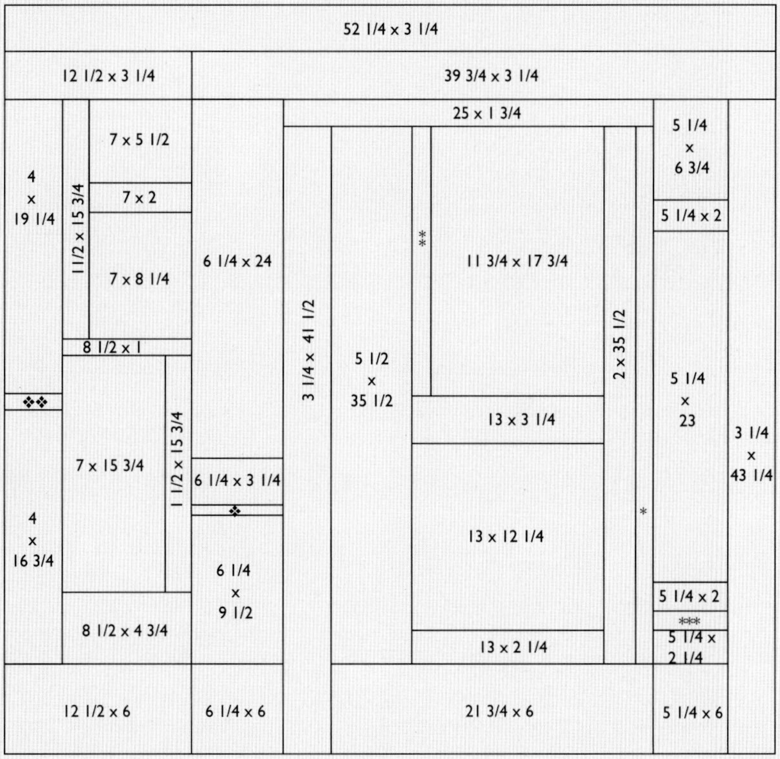

Top diagram (cm) labels:

- 132 x 8
- 32 x 8 | 100 x 8
- 63.5 x 4.5
- 4 x 40 | 18 x 14
- 18 x 5
- 13 x 17
- 13 x 5
- 10 x 49 | 18 x 21 | 16 x 60 | 30 x 45
- 8 x 105
- ** | 5 x 90
- 22 x 2.5
- 10 x 3 | 14 x 90 | 33 x 8 | 13 x 50.5
- 18 x 40 | * | 16 x 8 | 8 x 109
- ❖❖
- 10 x 42.5 | 33 x 31 | ❖
- 16 x 25
- 13 x 5
- 13 x 3
- 22 x 12 | 33 x 6 | 13 x 6
- 32 x 15 | 16 x 15 | 55.5 x 15 | 13 x 15

Legend:
❖ 3 x 90
❖❖ 16 x 1.5
* 4 x 40
** 3 x 45

All measurements are in inches.

Bottom diagram (inches) labels:

- 52 1/4 x 3 1/4
- 12 1/2 x 3 1/4 | 39 3/4 x 3 1/4
- 25 x 1 3/4
- 4 x 19 1/4 | 7 x 5 1/2
- 11 1/2 x 15 3/4 | 7 x 2
- 5 1/4 x 6 3/4
- 5 1/4 x 2
- 7 x 8 1/4 | 6 1/4 x 24 | 11 3/4 x 17 3/4
- 3 1/4 x 41 1/2
- ** | 2 x 35 1/2
- 8 1/2 x 1
- ❖❖ | 5 1/2 x 35 1/2 | 13 x 3 1/4 | 5 1/4 x 23
- 1 1/2 x 15 3/4 | 3 1/4 x 43 1/4
- 7 x 15 3/4 | 6 1/4 x 3 1/4
- ❖ | *
- 4 x 16 3/4 | 6 1/4 x 9 1/2 | 13 x 12 1/4
- 5 1/4 x 2
- ***
- 8 1/2 x 4 3/4 | 13 x 2 1/4 | 5 1/4 x 2 1/4
- 12 1/2 x 6 | 6 1/4 x 6 | 21 3/4 x 6 | 5 1/4 x 6

Legend:
❖ 6 1/4 x 1/2
❖❖ 4 x 1 1/4
* 1 1/4 x 35 1/2
** 1 1/4 x 17 3/4
*** 5 1/4 x 1 1/4

BENTE VOLD KLAUSEN

The day **Bente Vold Klausen** of Norway came across a copy of *Quilter's Newsletter Magazine* a friend brought back from the United States, her life changed forever. She managed to get more books and learned quilting by experimenting. Log Cabin quilts fascinated her, and

The Artist

she has even written a book about its variations and possibilities. ■ Her quilting evolved toward more creative work using stripes. She loves all shades of colors: strong and shiny, warm and mellow, intense and dark. She knows by experience to listen to her inner feelings and her mood of the day— she lets her intuition guide her. Bente feels it is important to use new combinations of elements we see. She considers herself very lucky to have the opportunity to express her feelings and communicate using textiles. ■ As she says, "I am from Norway, the Land of the Midnight Sun." Although she does not live in the north herself, the landscape and climate in this part of Norway are a strong part of her culture and identity, and are reflected in her work. ■ She is a teacher and a professional artist. Bente recently started publishing *Quiltemagasinet*, a Scandinavian magazine.

Stripes in Cross
34" x 37" (86 cm x 93 cm)
Bente has done a lot of strip piecing, and the cross is a graceful shape to work with.
Photo: Bente Vold Klausen

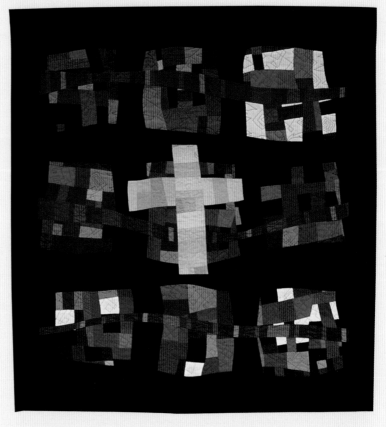

Thoughts of Despair

53" x 58" (135 cm x 148 cm)
When Bente is a bit depressed she loves to work with red, pink, and other bright colors. When she finished this quilt, her bad mood was long gone.

Photo: Bente Vold Klausen

The Gallery

In the Devil's Eye

28" x 28" (70 cm x 70 cm)
Bente loves the traditional Log Cabin technique and enjoys experimenting and inventing new variations. In this quilt, she varied the widths of the brightly colored, wavy strips.

Photo: Bente Vold Klausen

A Day at the Circus

52" x 55" (131 cm x 140 cm)
The circus was a fun, happy theme and gave Bente the opportunity to experiment more with the crazy patch technique. She sees the horse as a symbol of freedom and finds that in the circus arena, the horse behaves like a human being at a certain stage of life running in circles.

Photo: Bente Vold Klausen

Crossing Point

52" x 72" (132 cm x 183 cm)
Bente was inspired to made this quilt after a car ride through the western parts of Norway; with its mountain rivers (melting ice has an extremely green/blue color); deep, dark valleys; and black and red cottages clinging to the steep hillsides.

Photo: Bente Vold Klausen

The Project

Moonlight Makes No Life

96" x 81" (245 cm x 205 cm)
This quilt was made just after Bente moved to the countryside and was surrounded by large forested areas—thus the dark, heavy pine trees.

She is influenced by her surroundings, as well as the moon. The title of this quilt comes from a book written by a well-known Norwegian author who writes about feminism and social issues among the working class.

Photo: Bente Vold Klausen

his quilt is comprised of fabric scraps. Some of the scraps came from old dresses and some from fabrics Bente had been collecting for years. Use this project and its technique as inspiration; change the colors, the direction of the strips—use your own imagination and instinct.

The quilt consists of eight sections, each measuring 12" by 78" (30.5 cm x 198 cm) finished.

■ Two middle sections: dark blue/mauve and black

■ One section on each side of the middle section: dark blue/mauve, light blue/mauve, and black

■ Two sections on each side: light blue/mauve, medium blue/mauve, dark blue/mauve, and black

■ Some of the black pieces are highlighted with gold, some with white muslin.

■ Some corners have a touch of red as an accent.

Amounts are based on 45" (115 cm) fabric width.

■ Scraps of blue, mauve, red, white muslin, gold, and black with a touch of gold

■ Freezer paper or 7 yards (6.4 m) of muslin for foundation

■ 6 yards (5.5 m) for backing

■ 86" x 104" (218 cm x 264 cm) of batting

■ ⁵/₈ yard (60 cm) for binding

■ Template plastic (Option 2)

Cutting

Cut the freezer paper or muslin into eight 12¹/₂" x 78¹/₂" (32 cm x 199.5 cm) rectangles. Cut the gold fabrics into ¹/₂" (1.3 cm) strips. Cut the colored fabrics into 1⁵/₈" strips (4.1 cm). If you use scraps, the lengths will vary.

Assembly

Use a ¹/₄" (6 mm) seam allowance.

1. Draw irregular shapes on the eight paper or muslin rectangles, alternating the angles on each section.

2. Number each shape, starting with "1".

12 1/2"   12 1/2"
(32 cm)   (32 cm)

Draw shapes on the eight paper or muslin rectangles.

3. Choose either the foundation or template method. Cut the paper or muslin rectangles into pieces on the drawn lines. Use these shapes as foundations (Option 1), or trace, number, and cut the drawn shapes from template plastic (Option 2). *To avoid confusion, cut and piece one section of the quilt at a time.*

Foundation Method—Option 1

1. Sew a random combination of light blue/mauve, dark/blue mauve, medium blue/mauve, black/gold or white muslin strips covering the wrong side of each paper or muslin foundation. Be sure the strips extend at least ¹/₄" (6 mm) beyond the edge of the paper or muslin foundation. On each panel, try to use the same values or gradate them in a pleasant visual way. Press each strip open as it is added.

2. Trim around each shape, leaving a $1/4$" (6 mm) seam allowance.

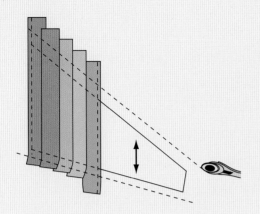

Sew strips on muslin foundations.

Template Method—Option 2

1. Sew the strips together as you wish. In each panel, try to use the same values or gradate them in a pleasant visual way. Press.

2. Place the template on the wrong side of each strip combination and draw around the template lines.

3. Trim around each shape, leaving a $1/4$" (6 mm) seam allowance.

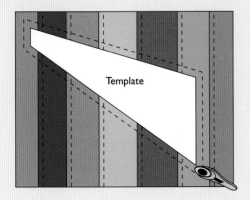

Trim.

Quilt Top Assembly

1. Sew each shape to the next one in numerical order, following the diagram on page 80.

2. Repeat for each of the eight sections. Remove the freezer paper if you have used it as a foundation.

3. Sew the sections together.

Finishing

1. Layer and quilt flames or any other pattern by hand or machine. It will probably be easier to machine quilt, since there are a lot of seams.

2. Bind with black.

Quilting Design

MARYLINE
COLLIOUD-ROBERT

The Artist

Since **Maryline Collioud-Robert**'s mother was a seamstress, Maryline had the opportunity to play with leftover fabrics of different colors and textures at an early age. ■ During the year Maryline spent in the United States as an exchange student, she slept under a beautiful basket quilt. Upon her return to Switzerland she started experimenting with patchwork without any idea where to start. In Europe at the time, it was difficult to find books on patchwork, so she soon set aside traditional blocks and started to develop her own designs. ■ She likes her quilts to work on three levels: the overall effect, which should work as a whole; the desire to analyze and discover the repeated unit and what changes occur from one unit to the next; and the ability of the fabrics and their variety to provide enjoyment. ■ Maryline gets her inspiration from every-day life: the wind in a wheat field, a particular flower blooming among others, a sudden change in the light in a room, unexpected color combinations in a street, or even a beautiful photograph. ■ She has exhibited her work in solo exhibitions and internationally in many prestigious venues. She also teaches in Switzerland and Germany.

Résonnances III
38" x 38" (97 cm x 97 cm)
This quilt belongs to a series of works where Maryline played with the colors of the color wheel and their interactions.
Photo: Maryline Collioud-Robert

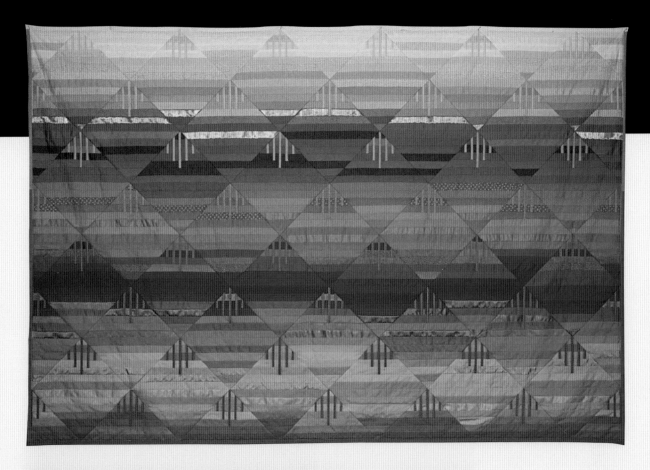

Suites et Contrastes II
(Series and Contrasts II)

67" x 44" (170 cm x 113 cm)
This quilt is part of a long series
in which Maryline always made
something happen in the top corner
of the tilted square. It allows endless
possibilities for color change and
light interaction.

Photo: Maryline Collioud-Robert

The Gallery

Chromatic

31" x 20" (80 cm x 50 cm)
Maryline has been fascinated by
Log Cabin blocks for a long time.
She has tried all kinds of
different ways to assemble
them —this one starts with
the small triangle.

Photo: Maryline Collioud-Robert

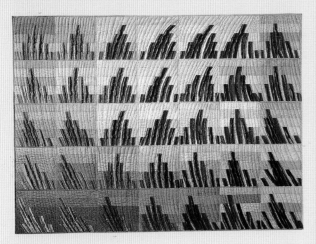

Quelques Herbes
(Some Herbs)

65" x 47" (165 cm x 119 cm)

Maryline wanted to give a more kinetic and spontaneous feeling to her quilts. Therefore, she freehand cut the grasses and attached them to the quilt using raw-edge appliqué.

Photo: Joël von Allmen

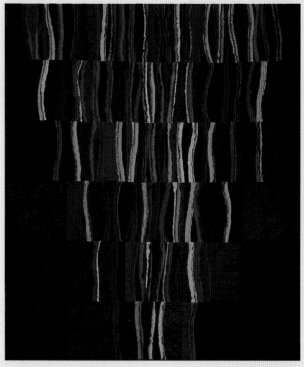

Nervures (Veins)

41" x 49" (104 cm x 124 cm)

Maryline got her inspiration watching her daughter knitting a scarf. She liked the contrast of the colors and the movement of the yarn. She decided to do something she has never done before—assemble with the seams showing on the right side of the quilt.

Photo: Maryline Collioud-Robert

Regard II (Gaze II)

61" x 61" (154 cm x 154 cm)

In this new series, Maryline
is using ordinary fabrics with
simple shapes and geometric
designs. Her intent is to play
with the effects of light.

Photo: Maryline Collioud-Robert

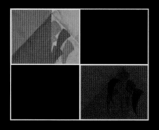

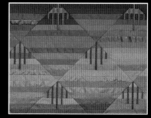

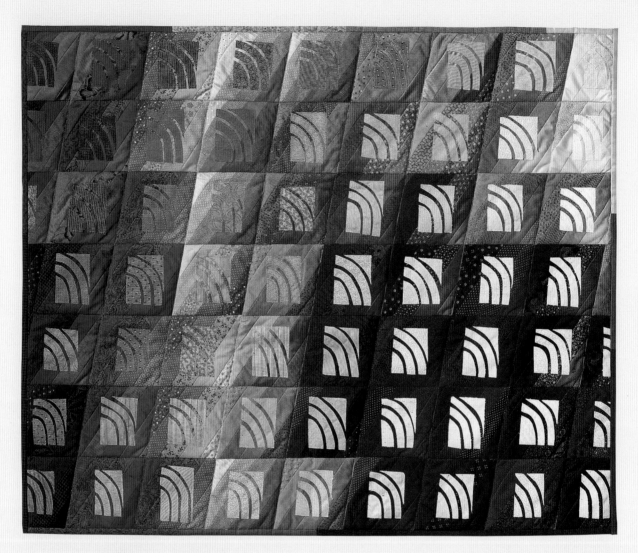

The Project

Rythme

34" x 28" (86 cm x 71 cm)

In this quilt, Maryline is influenced by everyday life and the repetitive tasks that we accomplish day after day.

Photo: Joël von Allmen

The design presents a metaphor. The white shapes symbolize a recurrance of everyday activity—the flow of pages of a diary, reminders of things we do daily. Yet even if we are in control of ourselves, we do not control the rest of the world. This is why the background is colorful and irregular.

Materials

Amounts are based on 45" (115 cm) fabric width.

Refer to the quilt photograph to help you choose fabrics, or create your own color scheme.

- 55 strips $1^1/_2$" x 8" (3.8 cm x 20.3 cm) of dark turquoise scraps
- 30 strips $1^1/_2$" x 8" (3.8 cm x 20.3 cm) of dark blue scraps
- 30 strips $1^1/_2$" x 8" (3.8 cm x 20.3 cm) of medium blue scraps
- 35 strips $1^1/_2$" x 8" (3.8 cm x 20.3 cm) of light blue scraps
- 20 strips $1^1/_2$" x 8" (3.8 cm x 20.3 cm) of lavender scraps
- 15 strips $1^1/_2$" x 8" (3.8 cm x 20.3 cm) of purple scraps
- 20 strips $1^1/_2$" x 8" (3.8 cm x 20.3 cm) of pink scraps
- 75 strips $1^1/_2$" x 8" (3.8 cm x 20.3 cm) of dark brown scraps
- 30 strips $1^1/_2$" x 8" (3.8 cm x 20.3 cm) of medium brown scraps
- 10 strips $1^1/_2$" x 8" (3.8 cm x 20.3 cm) of light brown scraps
- 62 rectangles $2^1/_2$" x $3^1/_2$" (6.4 cm x 8.9 cm) of light, contrasting fabrics for the appliqués
- 1 yard (1 m) of fusible adhesive
- 1 yard (1 m) for backing
- 34" x 40" (86.4 cm x 102 cm) of batting
- Scraps for binding
- Template plastic

Assembly

Use a $^1/_4$" (6mm) seam allowance.

1. Trace and cut out the template (page 89).

2. Choose five dark turquoise strips and stitch them together to form a stratum.

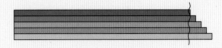

Stitch strips.

3. Continue sewing five like-color strips together until you have made 64 strata.

- 11 dark turquoise
- 6 dark blue
- 6 medium blue
- 7 light blue
- 4 lavender
- 3 purple
- 4 pink
- 15 dark brown
- 6 medium brown
- 2 light brown

4. Cut out each block using the template.

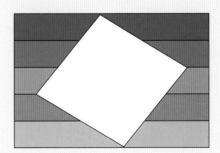

Cut using template.

5. Arrange the blocks following the diagram.

dark turq.	dark turquoise	medium blue	light blue	light blue	lavender	pink	medium brown	light brown
dark turq.	dark turquoise	medium blue	medium blue	lavender	pink	pink	medium brown	light brown
dk trq.	dark turquoise	dark blue	light blue	lavender	pink	medium brown	medium brown	medium brown
dark turquoise	dark blue	medium blue	light blue	purple	dark brown	dark brown	dark brown	med. brn
dark turquoise	dark blue	medium blue	lavender	purple	dark brown	dark brown	dark brown	dk brn
dark turquoise	dark blue	medium blue	light blue	purple	dark brown	dark brown	dark brown	drk brwn
dark turquoise	dark blue	dark blue	light blue	light blue	dark brown	dark brown	dark brown	dark brown

Quilt Assembly

6. Freehand cut sixty-two rectangles measuring approximately 2" x 3" (5.1 cm x 7.6 cm) from the fusible adhesive and fuse them to the light contrasting fabrics.

7. Choose one of the shapes at the right and freehand cut it from each rectangle.

Freehand cut shapes.

8. Remove the paper and fuse the shapes to each block. Machine stitch the shapes with a zigzag or a straight stitch.

9. Stitch the blocks together to form the quilt top, following the diagram at left. Press seams open.

10. Once the top is sewn together, trim into a rectangle.

Layer, quilt, and bind as desired.

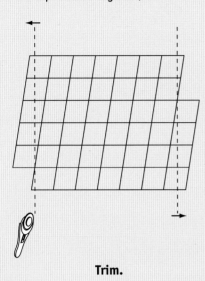

Trim.

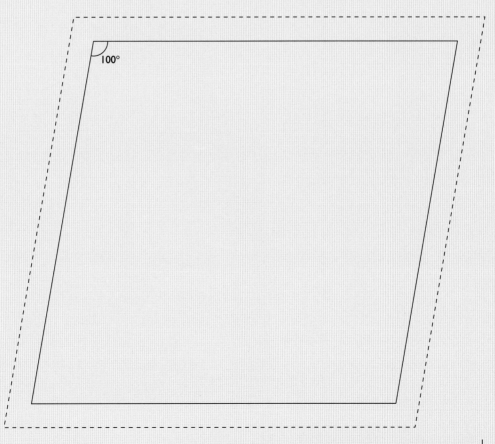

100°

MARIANNE HAENI

Marianne Haeni was born in Lucerne, and discovered quilting while visiting an exhibition of Amish quilts in Canada. She was immediately fascinated and, like most other quilters, began by making a few traditional

The Artist

quilts. Very soon though, after a few workshops with some of the great quilt artists, she started creating her own designs. ■ Thanks to a five-year stay in the United States, she was able to deepen her knowledge of quilting and realized that patchwork had become an art form in itself, in which the artist could pass on a message or simply be creative. In her work, she always expresses her feelings and her reaction to nature and other sources of inspiration. She also began to appreciate the social aspect of quilting. ■ During her childhood, she was fascinated by color and remembers arranging her colored pencils in their metal box in a thousand different ways. Marianne's quilts are about color. Design is an important aspect, but simple forms give her freedom to use her colors more than a sophisticated design would. That is why she always returns to squares and rectangles. ■ Marianne has exhibited in many places outside Switzerland, particularly in the United States and Japan.

The Scent of Spring
42" x 46" (106 cm x 117 cm)
Using the same size of blocks as in *Winter Freeze* and *Autumn Breeze*, Marianne took a big step forward and freed herself for new horizons—she decided to free cut the pieces of fabric of this quilt.

Photo: Marianne Haeni

Winter Freeze

42" x 46" (106 cm x 117 cm)
While using the same size
blocks as in *Autumn Breeze,*
Marianne chose the cool colors
and sharp shapes of the winter
season in Switzerland. Machine
pieced and machine quilted.
Commercial and hand-dyed
cotton fabrics.

Photo: Marianne Haeni

Autumn Breeze

42" x 46" (106 cm x 117 cm)
The first quilt in a series about
the four seasons. This theme
has always intrigued Marianne
because nature offers the widest
range of colors, which change
throughout the year. This quilt
is her own interpretation of the
Log Cabin block. Machine pieced
and machine quilted. Commercial
and hand-dyed cotton fabrics.

Photo: Marianne Haeni

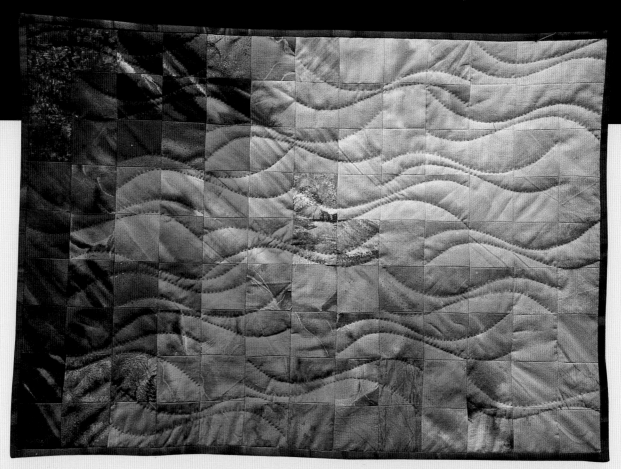

Water

24" x 17" (60 cm x 42 cm)

Wind

24" x 17" (60 cm x 42 cm)

Fire

24" x 17" (60 cm x 42 cm)

The elements, like the seasons, are a constant inspiration for Marianne. Each individual square is like a brushstroke that a painter applies to his painting.

These three quilts are part of the same series and were made with the same inspiration. Machine pieced, hand quilted.

Photos: Marianne Haeni

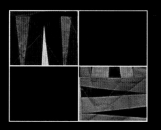

The Project

Summer Heat

42" x 46" (106 cm x 117 cm)

Marianne wanted to express the feeling of lying in the sun by the seashore, enjoying the warmth of the sand and relaxing.

Photo: Marianne Haeni

Summer reminds Marianne of the sea. Dark blue fabrics represent the coolness of the water and light blues, the sky getting misty at the end of a hot day. The fish and seaweed are interpreted with contrasting bright colors in reverse appliqué.

Materials

Amounts are based on 45" (115 cm) fabric width.

■ ¹/₂ yard (46 cm) each of six different blue-green fabrics, from light to dark for the background, borders, and binding (gradated fabrics from light to dark are ideal)

■ Scraps of contrasting reds and yellows for the seaweed and fish

■ 1¹/₂ yards (1.4 m) for backing

■ 48" x 52" (122 cm x 132 cm) of batting

Cutting

Cut 5" (12.7 cm) strips for blocks. Cut the strips into rectangles and squares following the diagram. Cut two 5" x 32" (12.7 cm x 81.3 cm) strips for the side borders and two 5" x 46¹/₂" (12.7 cm x 118 cm) strips for the top and bottom borders.

Assembly

Use a ¹/₄" (6 mm) seam allowance.

1. Place the background rectangles and squares on a design wall following the diagram.

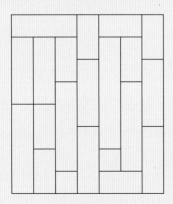

Quilt Diagram

2. Once you are happy with the arrangement, draw freehand designs on top of the background. These designs can float or disappear.

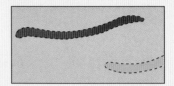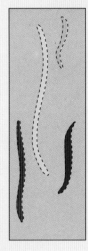

Draw freehand designs.

3. Choose one of your accent colors and cut a piece so it overlaps the freehand design ¹/₂" (12 mm) on each side. Lay it underneath the freehand design right side up, and pin.

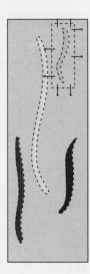

Lay accent fabric underneath freehand design.

4. Sew along the drawn lines with a zigzag stitch, working on the right side of the background fabric. The threads should match the background fabric. Proceed the same way for all the designs.

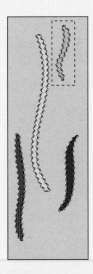

Zigzag stitch on drawn lines.

5. With sharp, pointed scissors trim the top fabric just inside of the zigzag stitches. Be careful not to damage the bottom (accent) fabric, or cut the stitches.

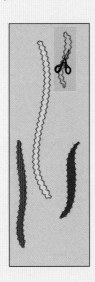

Trim inside zigzag stitches.

6. Trim all excess bottom (accent) fabric to within ½" (12 mm) of the stitches and return the block to the design wall. Proceed the same way for all the blocks.

7. Assemble the blocks following the diagram. Press the seams open.

8. If necessary, draw more freehand designs overlapping the seams of the assembled blocks to give the surface a third dimension and to make the seams less obvious.

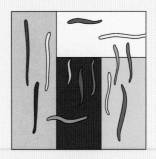

Add freehand designs overlapping the seams.

9. Attach the borders: the sides first, then the top and bottom.

Finishing

1. Layer and machine quilt with a dark green-blue thread in curves reminiscent of sea waves.

2. Add binding.

C. JUNE BARNES

June Barnes' work is influenced by growing up in Africa. Because of the strong light in Africa, she sees color in a very clear way and is particularly drawn to bright, strong colors. ■ June has a particular fascination with

The Artist

wildlife and nature; design from the Baroque and Jacobean eras; ancient civilizations such as Maya and Inca; architectural structures, both modern and ancient; and the ethnic peoples of Africa and Australia. All these things influence her quilts. She is a great advocate of the idea that there are no rules beyond those of basic workmanship. ■ June sews extensively with men's shirts and ties, making quilts which are donated to charities. Her collection of ties is massive, probably over 10,000! ■ Quiltmaking not only satisfies her creativity but she also uses it as a medium to draw attention to issues of concern in the world. This is reflected in her quilt *The Crude Sea,* which is a protest against oil spillage from tankers. ■ June has exhibited her quilts in Britain, as well as in other areas of Europe and the United States, and has won many awards.

The Crude Sea

62" x 67" (158 cm x 170 cm)
The Crude Sea was made as a protest against the spillage of the Seam Empress' crude oil when she ran aground. The result was mindless destruction of birds and sea life due to the pollution of the sea and shoreline. The beads remind us that the sea is a jewel which we should have more respect for. Machine pieced and quilted.

Photo: Robert Claxton

Cloudcuckooland

72" x 48" (183 cm x 122 cm)

June attended a workshop by Linda Straw where she learned Linda's technique of machine appliqué from the back of the work. This quilt was the result of that workshop.

June wanted to represent the wonderful world of birds in caricature fashion, but found that the birds were becoming more and more realistic. Machine appliquéd and machine quilted.

Photo: Robert Claxton

The Gallery

Steady Progress

72" x 48" (183 cm x 122 cm)

This quilt explores the progressive development of a block, a variation of Shoo-fly. The quarter block at the top left represents the goal in life. The quarter block at the bottom right is a reminder of the humble beginnings.

Photo: Robert Claxton

Guinea Fowl (Hanga)

24" x 24" (61 cm x 61 cm)

This quilt was made for Annette Claxton. It is in effect an "apple for the teacher," featuring June's favorite African bird — the guinea fowl. Machine pieced, appliquéd, and quilted.

Photo: Robert Claxton

Take One:
Happy Medium

72" x 48" (183 cm x 122 cm)
This quilt began with a simple block arrangement, but the color scheme has been allowed to expand and develop. The simple beginnings of this quilt have encouraged the enhancement of secondary patterns. There is warmth, interest, and relaxed control: a combination that we perhaps strive for.

Photo: Robert Claxton

Take One: Letting Go

72" x 48" (183 cm x 122 cm)
The rules have been relaxed, and the colors diverted from the plain fabrics into an assortment of patterned fabrics. The result is a quilt influenced by African-American style. Chaos rules!

There is an element of fun here, but we feel uncomfortable because our conditioning dictates conformity. The quilt reminds June of her house — at times fairly chaotic!

Photo: C. June Barnes

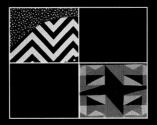

The Project

Desert Sunset

36" x 60" (91 cm x 152 cm)

This quilt was made using fabrics dyed in a workshop with Jan Myers-Newbury. Machine pieced and quilted.

Photo: C. June Barnes

Materials

Amounts are based on 45" (115 cm) fabric width.

- $3/8$ yard (34 cm) each of five brown fabrics, gradated from light (brown #1) to medium dark (brown #5)
- $3/8$ yard (34 cm) each of five yellow fabrics, gradated from light (yellow #1) to dark (yellow #5)
- $1/4$ yard (23 cm) black for inner border
- $1^1/4$ yards (1.1 m) dark brown for outer border and binding
- $1^3/4$ yards (1.6 m) for backing
- 46" x 56" (117 cm x 142 cm) of batting

Cutting

- Six $1^1/2$" x 45" (3.8 cm x 115 cm) strips from each yellow fabric
- Six $1^1/2$" x 45" (3.8 cm x 115 cm) strips from each brown gradated fabric

Assembly

Use a $1/4$" (6 mm) seam allowance.

Yellow Gradated Units

1. Beginning with yellow #5 (dark), sew the strips together following the diagram (Unit 1). You will use four strips of each yellow fabric.

Unit 1

2. Beginning with yellow #5 (dark), sew the strips together, following the diagram (Unit 2). You will use two strips of each yellow fabric.

Unit 2

Brown Gradated Units

1. Beginning with brown #1 (light), sew the strips together, following the diagram (Unit 3). You will use three strips of each brown gradated fabric.

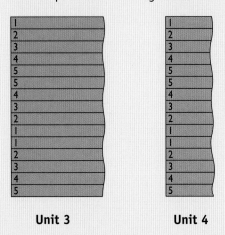

Unit 3   Unit 4

2. Cut a 16" (40.6 cm) strip from each of the fifteen remaining brown gradated strips. Beginning with brown #1 (light), sew the strips together following the diagram (Unit 4).

3. Using one of each color of the remaining strips, sew the strips together, following the diagram (Unit 5).

Unit 5

4. Following the diagrams, cut the pieces indicated. All cut angles are either 45° or 90°. H is four strips high and I is eight strips wide.

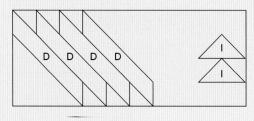

Unit 1

Unit 2

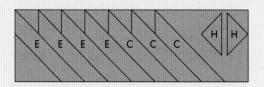

Unit 3

Unit 4

Unit 5

5. Assemble the quilt top, one quarter at a time following the diagram on page 103.

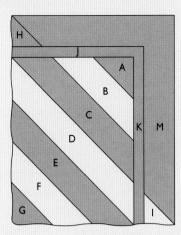

Quilt Construction

Inner Border

1. Cut two $1^1/_2$" x 45" (3.8 cm x 115 cm) strips for the top and bottom borders (J). Add to the quilt top (to be mitered).

2. Cut two $1^1/_2$" x 45" (3.8 cm x 115 cm) strips for the side borders (K). Add to the quilt top and miter the corners.

Outer Border

1. Cut one $4^1/_2$" x 45" (11.4 cm x 115 cm) strip for the top border (L). Cut in half crosswise.

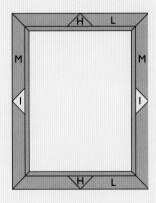

Outer Border

2. Lay one strip on each side of an H triangle. Cut a 45° angle on one end of each border strip.

3. Sew one L strip to each side of H. Press seams toward L.

4. Repeat steps 1–3 for the bottom border.

5. Add top and bottom borders to the quilt top (to be mitered).

6. Cut two $4^1/_2$" x 45" (11.4 cm x 115 cm) strips for one of the side borders (M).

7. Lay one strip on each side of an I triangle cut previously. Cut a 45° angle on one end of each border strip, as in step 2.

8. Sew one M strip to each side of I. Press seams toward I.

9. Repeat steps 6–8 for the other side border.

10. Add to the quilt top and miter the corners.

Quilt Assembly

Layer, quilt, and bind as desired.

JANICE GUNNER

When **Janice Gunner** began making traditional quilts in the United Kingdom, it was difficult to find fabrics, books, or any materials relating to patchwork. After attending the national City and Guilds diploma courses

The Artist

in patchwork and quilting, which she began taking in 1991, she evolved into more contemporary quiltmaking. She continued on and completed Part II in 1997. She also attended workshops taught by many internationally renowned teachers in the United Kingdom and the United States. ■ Janice plans to continue developing her work in as many diverse ways as possible, including using other textile media to add interest and texture to her quilts, and is continuing to expand a new technique of manipulated fabric patchwork she created during City and Guilds Patchwork and Quilting, Part II. ■ Janice has exhibited her work in major exhibitions, both at home and abroad, for many years, winning numerous awards. Most recently she shared second prize for Technical Excellence in the Charles Henry Foyle Textile Award at the Forge Mill Needle Museum, Redditch, England; won first prize in the Expressive Quilts category at the European Quilt Championship 1999 for her quilt *Skye Escape I;* and was granted the Jewel Pearce Patterson Scholarship for Best International Quilt Teacher 1999.

Summer Fuchsia Show

24" (61 cm) equilateral triangle

Inspired by the colors seen at a flower show, Janice experimented with the textured triangles technique she created.

This quilt is part of the 1990 collection of the Quilters Guild of the British Isles.

Photo: Janice Gunner

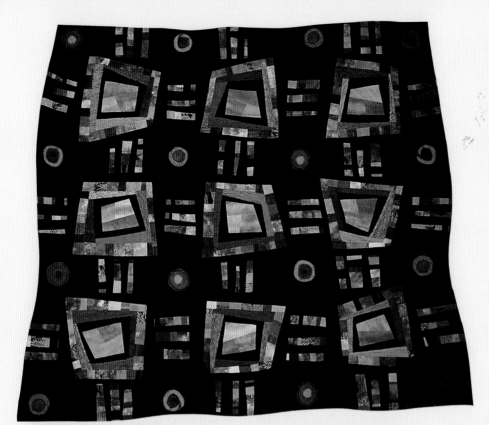

Skye Escape III

50" x 48" (122 cm x 127 cm)

The third in a series inspired by
the Isle of Skye in Scotland.

Photo: Janice Gunner

The Gallery

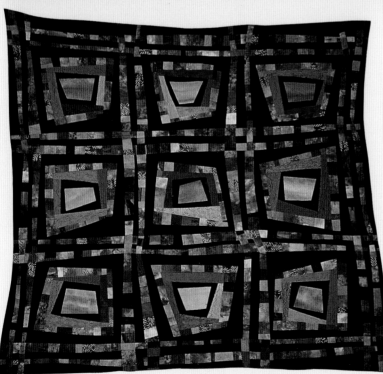

Skye Escape II

50" x 50" (127 cm x 127 cm)

The second in a series inspired
by the Isle of Skye in Scotland.

Photo: Janice Gunner

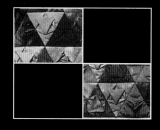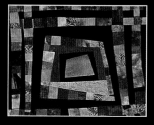

The Project

Siam Sizzle

21" x 21" (53 cm x 53 cm)
The colors in this quilt were
inspired by Thailand. The name
Siam Sizzle refers to the old
name for Thailand and the
wonderful, vibrant colors used.

The quilt was awarded third
place in the theme category
"East Meets West" at the Great
British Quilt Festival in
Harrogate, England in 1997.
Thai silk and cotton fabrics.

Photo: Janice Gunner

he design for this quilt was inspired by shapes taken from a collage made during a workshop with Siripan Kidd, a quilting friend who was born in Thailand. The colors represent the green rice fields, orange Buddhist monk robes, Golden Temples, red poppies grown in the Golden Triangle, and the blue Andaman Sea.

Materials

Amounts are based on a 45" (115 cm) fabric width.

- ¹/₄ yard (23 cm) each of red, yellow, green, and orange fabrics
- ³/₄ yard (70 cm) azure blue for borders and binding
- ³/₄ yard (70 cm) for backing
- 27" x 27" (69 cm x 69 cm) of batting
- Template plastic

Assembly

Use ¹/₄" (6 mm) seam allowance.

1. Trace templates onto template plastic using a fine-line permanent black pen. Number and mark grain lines on each piece.

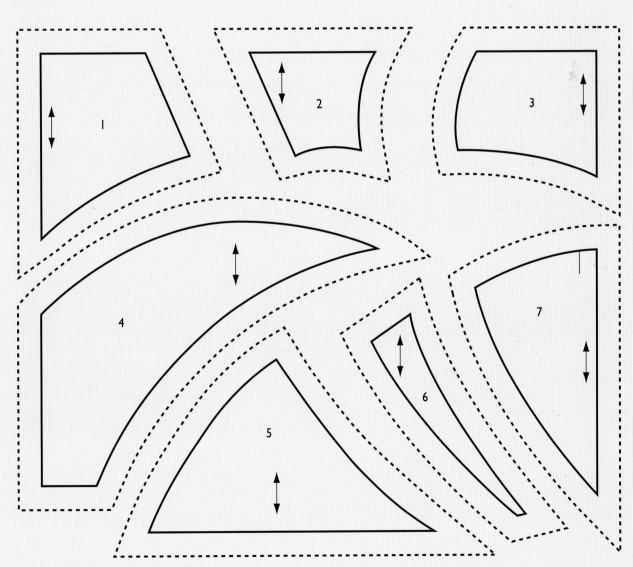

2. Place templates right side down on wrong side of fabric, draw around each template, and cut 16 of each shape as follows, adding ¼" (6 mm) seam allowance.

Red fabric   templates #2 and #6

Green fabric   template #4

Orange fabric   templates #1 and #5

Yellow fabric   templates #3 and #7

3. Join pieces 1, 2, and 3 stitching on the marked lines.

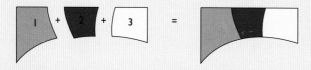

Join 1, 2, and 3.

4. Join pieces 5, 6, and 7.

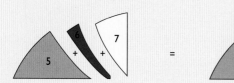

Join 5, 6, and 7.

5. From the right side, press seams to one side. Clip curved seam allowance on the wrong side. This will help the seams to lie flat.

6. Join top section (1-2-3) to curve of piece 4. Press and clip seam.

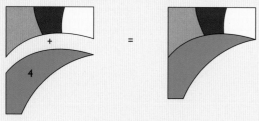

Join 1-2-3 to 4.

7. Join lower section (5-6-7) to lower curve of piece 4. Press and clip seam.

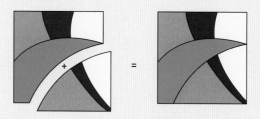

Join 5-6-7 to 4.

8. Complete each block in this way. The block should measure 4" (10 cm) finished. Join blocks as shown in diagram. You could rotate the blocks differently to produce a different design.

Quilt Assembly

9. Press the seams of each row in opposite directions so the seams butt together neatly. Join rows to form the center panel. Press.

10. Using azure fabric cut borders as follows:

■ One $16^1/2$" x $4^1/2$" (42 cm x 11.4 cm) strip for top border

■ Two 18" x $4^1/2$" (45.7 cm x 11.4 cm) strip for left side and bottom borders

■ One $22^1/2$" x $4^1/2$" (57.2 cm x 11.4 cm) strip for right side border

11. Cut each of these strips into the wedge shape required by placing the edge of your ruler on the top *right* corner of the fabric strip, then pivoting the ruler down on the *left* side until the 2" (5.1 cm) mark on the ruler is level with the bottom left corner of the fabric strip. Rotary cut the angle on the fabric with the ruler in this position. You will use only the bottom section of the strip for the border.

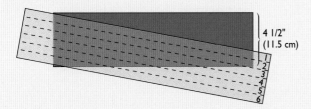

Cut border strips into wedge shapes.

12. Sew borders onto center panel—top, left side, bottom, and right side (as in the log cabin construction), pressing seams toward each border.

13. Press entire piece and square up if necessary.

1. Using invisible thread for top thread in the machine and cotton thread on the bobbin, free-motion machine quilt the center panel.

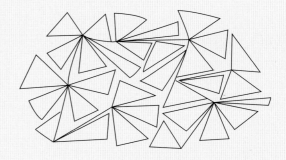

Quilting Design

2. The border is quilted with random wavy lines to represent the waves on the sea. Stitch outward from the center panel to the edge of the quilt and back again.

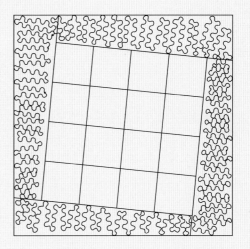

Quilting Design for Border

3. Cut straight bindings from the azure fabric $1^1/2$" (3.8 cm) wide. Bind as desired.

Farb Stoff

Heide Stoll Weber
Lersnerstrasse 26
60322 Frankfurt/Main
Germany
Phone/fax: + 49 69 59 03 30
email: hsw.sw@t-online.de
Hand-dyed cotton, fine poplin fabrics with
multicolor effects, and dyeing classes

Susan E. Seagram

Ancienne Gare
21410 Gissey sur Ouche
France
Phone: + 33 3 80 23 60 00
Fax: + 33 3 80 49 09 34
email: seagram @ claranet.fr
Hand-dyed cotton, Cotton Club subscription
service, special order hand-dyed fabrics, workshops, Indigo weekends.

Sweet Arts

10, route de Maron
33370 Fargues Saint Hilaire
France
Phone/fax: + 33 5 56 68 36 71
Boutis supplies, including 6 oz. fine cotton
cording

Der Stoffladen

Cira Stoffladen
Bahnhofstrasse 4
91154 Roth
Germany
Phone: + 49 9171/61156
Fax: + 49 97171/88371
Marimekko fabrics

Nielsen McNally

6 Eggars Hill
Aldershot
Hampshire Gull 3N9
United Kingdom
Phone: + 44 (1252) 326416
Fax: + 44 (1252) 334490
Marimekko fabrics

Cotton Patch Mail Order

3405 Hall Lane, Dept. CTB
Lafayette, CA 94549
USA
Phone: 800-835-4418   925-283-7883
email: quiltusa@yahoo.com
Web: www.quiltusa.com
Quilting supplies, including 6 oz. fine cotton
cording for boutis

Quilters' Resource

P.O. Box 148850
Chicago, IL 60614
USA
Phone: 773-278-5695
Fax: 773-278-1348
Wholesale only
Distributor of quilting and needle art supplies;
including 6 oz. fine cotton cording for boutis.

GÜL LAPORTE

Thirty years ago, Gül was a marketing executive in one of ITT's French subsidiaries. She never thought that one day she would be so involved in quilting—teaching and lecturing throughout Europe. ■ Gül now lives in

The Author

France, but has lived in Algeria, Syria, Greece, the United States, and the United Kingdom. She is fluent in French, English, and Spanish, and conversant in Greek. ■ She originally discovered quilting in 1981 in Houston. Upon returning to Europe, she continued to quilt and soon began teaching throughout Europe, including workshops at Quilt Expo V in Lyon and Expo VI in Innsbruck. While visiting important shows in Europe she met many European artists with whom she had the opportunity

to share and exchange ideas. She also realized that European artists were not very well known in the United States and other parts of the world, and thought it would be a good idea to write a book about a few of them so these artists could share their inspiration with other quilters. ■ Gül exhibited her work in a solo exhibition in Paris in 1992 and since then has been invited several times to show her quilts in national and international events. Her first book, *Patchwork d'hier et d'aujourd'hui*, co-written with Monique Giraud, was published in 1996 in French (Editions Fleurus).

An Amish Adventure: 2nd Edition, Roberta Horton

Anatomy of a Doll: The Fabric Sculptor's Handbook, Susanna Oroyan

Appliqué 12 Easy Ways! : Charming Quilts, Giftable Projects & Timeless Techniques, Elly Sienkiewicz

Art & Inspirations: Ruth B. McDowell, Ruth B. McDowell

The Art of Silk Ribbon Embroidery, Judith Baker Montano

The Art of Classic Quiltmaking, Harriet Hargrave and Sharyn Craig

The Artful Ribbon, Candace Kling

At Home with Patrick Lose: Colorful Quilted Projects, Patrick Lose

Baltimore Beauties and Beyond (Volume I), Elly Sienkiewicz

Basic Seminole Patchwork, Cheryl Greider Bradkin

The Best of Baltimore Beauties, Elly Sienkiewicz

Beyond the Horizon: Small Landscape Appliqué, Valerie Hearder

Color From the Heart: Seven Great Ways to Make Quilts with Colors You Love, Gai Perry

Crazy Quilt Handbook, Judith Montano

Crazy with Cotton, Diana Leone

Curves in Motion: Quilt Designs & Techniques, Judy B. Dales

Deidre Scherer: Work in Fabric & Thread, Deidre Scherer

Designing the Doll: From Concept to Construction, Susanna Oroyan

Easy Pieces: Creative Color Play with Two Simple Blocks, Margaret Miller

Elegant Stitches: An Illustrated Stitch Guide & Source Book of Inspiration, Judith Baker Montano

Everything Flowers: Quilts from the Garden, Jean and Valori Wells

Exploring Machine Trapunto: New Dimensions, Hari Walner

Fabric Shopping with Alex Anderson, Seven Project to Help You: Make, Successful Choices, Build Your Confidence, Add to Your Fabric Stash, Alex Anderson

Faces & Places: Images in Appliqué, Charlotte Warr Andersen

Fancy Appliqué: 12 Lessons to Enhance Your Skills, Elly Sienkiewicz

Fantastic Fabric Folding: Innovative Quilting Projects, Rebecca Wat

Fantastic Figures: Ideas & Techniques Using the New Clays, Susanna Oroyan

Focus on Features: Life-like Portrayals in Appliqué, Charlotte Warr Andersen

Forever Yours: Wedding Quilts, Clothing & Keepsakes, Amy Barickman

Freddy's House: Brilliant Color in Quilts, Freddy Moran

Free Stuff for Collectors on the Internet, Judy Heim and Gloria Hansen

Free Stuff for Crafty Kids on the Internet, Judy Heim and Gloria Hansen

Free Stuff for Gardeners on the Internet, Judy Heim and Gloria Hansen

Free Stuff for Quilters on the Internet, 2nd Ed., Judy Heim and Gloria Hansen

Free Stuff for Sewing Fanatics on the Internet, Judy Heim and Gloria Hansen

Free Stuff for Stitchers on the Internet, Judy Heim and Gloria Hansen

From Fiber to Fabric: The Essential Guide to Quiltmaking Textiles, Harriet Hargrave

Hand Quilting with Alex Anderson: Six Projects for Hand Quilters, Alex Anderson

Heirloom Machine Quilting, Third Edition, Harriet Hargrave

Imagery on Fabric, Second Edition, Jean Ray Laury

Impressionist Palette, Gai Perry

Impressionist Quilts, Gai Perry

Jacobean Rhapsodies: Composing with 28 Appliqué Designs, Patricia B. Campbell and Mimi Ayars

Judith Baker Montano: Art & Inspirations, Judith Baker Montano

Kaleidoscopes: Wonders of Wonder, Cozy Baker

Kaleidoscopes & Quilts, Paula Nadelstern

Make Any Block Any Size, Joen Wolfrom

Mariner's Compass Quilts, New Directions, Judy Mathieson

Mastering Machine Appliqué, Harriet Hargrave

Mastering Quilt Marking: Marking Tools & Techniques, Choosing Stencils, Matching Borders & Corners, Pepper Cory

Michael James: Art & Inspirations, Michael James

The New England Quilt Museum Quilts: Featuring the Story of the Mill Girls. With Instructions for 5 Heirloom Quilts, Jennifer Gilbert

The New Sampler Quilt, Diana Leone

On the Surface: Thread Embellishment & Fabric Manipulation, Wendy Hill

Patchwork Persuasion: Fascinating Quilts from Traditional Designs, Joen Wolfrom

Patchwork Quilts Made Easy, Jean Wells (co-published with Rodale Press, Inc.)

The Photo Transfer Handbook: Snap It, Print It, Stitch It!, Jean Ray Laury

Pieced Clothing Variations, Yvonne Porcella

Pieced Flowers, Ruth B. McDowell

Pieced Roman Shades: Turn Your Favorite Quilt Patterns into Window Hangings, Terrell Sundermann

Pieces of an American Quilt, Patty McCormick

Piecing: Expanding the Basics, Ruth B. McDowell

Plaids & Stripes: The Use of Directional Fabrics in Quilts, Roberta Horton

Quilt It for Kids; 11 Projects, Sports, Fantasy & Animal Themes, Quilts for Children of All Ages, Pam Bono

Quilts for Fabric Lovers, Alex Anderson

Quilts from the Civil War: Nine Projects, Historical Notes, Diary Entries, Barbara Brackman

Quilts, Quilts, and More Quilts! Diana McClun and Laura Nownes

Recollections, Judith Baker Montano

RIVA: If Ya Wanna Look Good Honey, Your Feet Gotta Hurt..., Ruth Reynolds

Rotary Cutting with Alex Anderson: Tips, Techniques, and Projects, Alex Anderson

Rx for Quilters: Stitcher-Friendly Advice for Every Body, Susan Delaney Mech, M.D.

Say It with Quilts, Diana McClun and Laura Nownes

Scrap Quilts: The Art of Making Do, Roberta Horton

Shadow Quilts: Easy-to-Design Multiple Image Quilts, Patricia Magaret and Donna Slusser

Simply Stars: Quilts that Sparkle, Alex Anderson

Six Color World: Color, Cloth, Quilts & Wearables, Yvonne Porcella

Skydyes: A Visual Guide to Fabric Painting, Mickey Lawler

Small Scale Quiltmaking: Precision, Proportion, and Detail, Sally Collins

Soft-Edge Piecing, Jinny Beyer

Special Delivery Quilts, Patrick Lose

Start Quilting with Alex Anderson: Six Projects for First-Time Quilters, Alex Anderson

Stripes in Quilts, Mary Mashuta

Through the Garden Gate: Quilters and Their Gardens, Jean and Valori Wells

Tradition with a Twist: Variations on Your Favorite Quilts, Blanche Young and Dalene Young Stone

Trapunto by Machine, Hari Walner

Travels with Peaky and Spike: Doreen Speckmann's Quilting Adventures, Doreen Speckmann

The Visual Dance: Creating Spectacular Quilts, Joen Wolfrom

Wild Birds: Designs for Appliqué & Quilting, Carol Armstrong

Wildflowers: Designs for Appliqué & Quilting, Carol Armstrong

Willowood: Further Adventures in Buttonhole Stitch Appliqué, Jean Wells

Women of Taste: A Collaboration Celebrating Quilt Artists and Chefs, Girls, Inc.

Yvonne Porcella: Art & Inspirations, Yvonne Porcella

For more information write for a free catalog:
C&T Publishing, Inc.
P.O. Box 1456
Lafayette, CA 94549
(800) 284-1114
http://www.ctpub.com
e-mail: ctinfo@ctpub.com

For quilting supplies:
Cotton Patch Mail Order
3405 Hall Lane, Dept. CTB
Lafayette, CA 94549
e-mail: quiltusa@yahoo.com
web: www.quiltusa.com
(800) 835-4418
(925) 283-7883